THE MEDIOCRE MIRACLE

Ritchie R Thomas Jr

Copyright © 2020 Ritchie R Thomas Jr

All rights reserved

Acknowledgments

To God, I thank you, I need you, I love you, sorry it took me so long…

To Charleston who raised the boy & Atlanta who raised the man.

The 2008 Recession	Cory/Debi
Shelby Gene	Wayne/Kelsey
Mildred	Gabby/Natheer
My Mom	My Dad
Kip	Coach David Smith
Richard/Angie	Wolfgang
Kenneth	Sugarbear Monster
Mean Martha	Mr. Butler
Dr. Sparks	Hayden
Uncle Bobby	Auron Xavier
Uncle William	Team Whaley
Uncle Ola	Woody
Uncle Allen	SSG Coen

SSG Madero
PFC Harris, Blue Falcon
Dr. Kimbro
Sue Bee
Jim Rohn
T. Robbins
Eric Thomas
Les Brown
Wayne Dyer
Mel Robbins
Earl Nightingale
Lovingbug J
ATV Bible Study Crew
Aunt Wanda
Brittney/Tim

James 'Lefty' Brown
Jerome & Fred
Welvin/Avalon
Abeer/Keyana
The Wilson Sisters
The Great Lord Thaddeus of the Land
Brandon
Dale Bronner
The Lovett School
Trav
The Jaimster
Kathy Baby
GMA Team
SOCSOUTH

<u>ETA Family</u>:
Big Bro Kantis
Aunt Val
Uncle Kendall
ET/CJ

I am all that I have been. You've all been a part of my journey, there are simply not enough words...

To the girl that I've loved since 4th grade, my wife, Tyesha…

Contents

Acknowledgments iii
Introduction ix
Life Lesson 1: Driving Without a Map 1
Life Lesson 2: Get Out of Your Head 6
Life Lesson 3: The Necessary Struggle: 9
Life Lesson 4: The Ultimate Distraction 22
Life Lesson 5: The Mental Diet 33
Life Lesson 6: The Rule of 168 36
Life Lesson 7: When the Student is Ready............... 41
Life Lesson 8: Your Life Plan 46
Life Lesson 9: But the Company Didn't… 92
Life Lesson 10: Why You Make What You Make 99
Life Lesson 11: The Mediocre Miracle 131
Resources: 142
About the Author 145

Introduction

At the time of publishing this book, I am 37 years old, which equates to 13,505 days on this Earth. If I was even halfway paying attention and my math is right, then hopefully, I've learned 13,505 lessons. Of those lessons, the biggest issue I see us all cope with is our struggle, clarity, life transitions, and most of all, coming to grips with our place on this planet.

Have you ever struggled with something: i.e. school, a relationship, a crappy car, a crappy job, career, etc., and try to make sense of it? I continue to talk to folks who are in different phases of life and have no clue why they are there. They have no clue what their purpose is or have no clue what they want to do in life. They have no personal mission or self-defined marching orders.

They have no real answer to why they stayed at the job they just 'like' for over ten years. I run across countless people, young and old, who simply seem unsatisfied with:

where they are
who they are
and ever more so unsatisfied with ***where they are going*** and ***who they are becoming.***

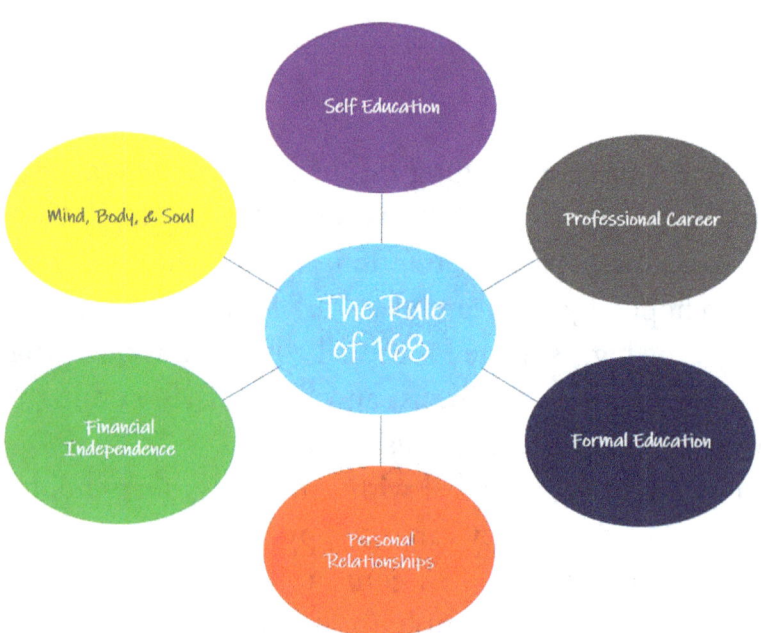

Therefore, I put together a piece of work to assist in providing clarity in your transformational journey. It is my hope to get you from where you are, to where you want to be, and most importantly, I hope that reading this helps you discover *who you need to become* to get there.

Introduction

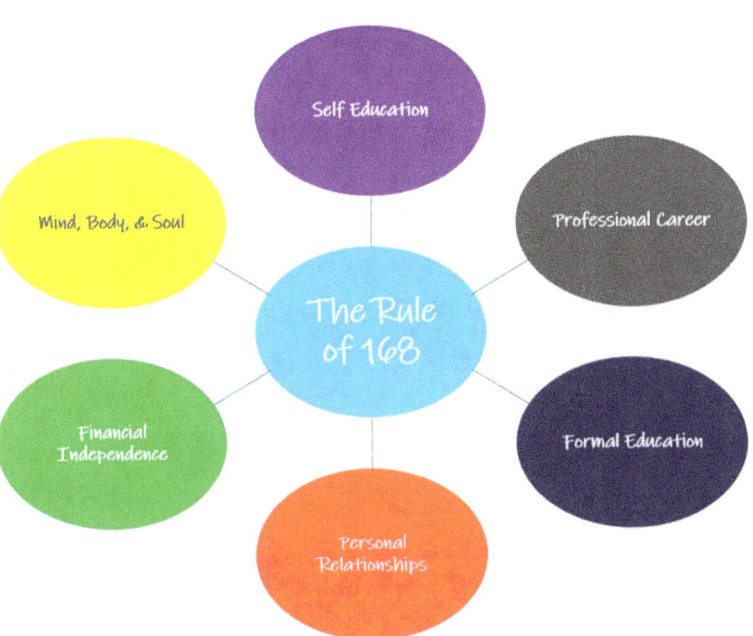

Life Lesson 1

Driving Without a Map

Distractions

It's hard to do something while distracted and can be likened to running a race while worrying about others in the race. It would be like participating in the Olympics and losing, but saying, "Hey, we have the best uniforms." We are distracted by Instagram, our family, Monday Night Football, College Gameday, 'insert favorite celebrity,' Netflix, Game of Thrones, 'where will LeBron James play next year,' the presidential election, a job you hate, etc.

It's almost as if we look for any reason to distract us from our hearts.

Driving from Atlanta to LA (map scenario)

I'd like to give you a riddle if you'll humor me. Let's say you're driving from Atlanta, Ga and everything you'd love to have in life awaits you in Los Angeles, California.

Your dream family scenario…
Your dream house…
Your dream spouse...
Your dream career…
Your dream business...
Your dream financial situation…

and anything else that you can imagine having your dream life, but you must drive from Atlanta to LA to live out your dreams, and of course, there are several stipulations.

There is no map to help get you there.

There is no GPS (No Google, Waze, or Siri) (:|).

There is no cell phone, in fact, yours has just been destroyed, and the battery is dead.

There are no road or street signs, so you cannot tell if you're going North, South, East, or West or cannot positively identify which highway or interstate you're on.

Every time that you stop and ask someone for directions or guidance, they either give you the shoulder shrug response, as in, "I don't know what to tell you," or they send you in the wrong direction.

There is the occasional convoy that drives by and you may follow them, but you'll soon realize upon asking, that they may not even know where they're going exactly (or what route they are to take to get there).

There is also horrible weather on this trip. In fact, it is raining profusely or at least cloudy enough that you cannot see the sky.

Of course, this is all a life scenario. Often it feels like we are traveling aimlessly, with no real destination, we have no real map, no GPS, no clear signs, our friends and family cannot necessarily tell us where to go and how to get there. In the event that they do offer advice or guidance, it may appear that they are giving us *their* opinion of where *they'd* like us to go, which takes us further off our true path. We may get lost by following the crowd and even if we do get somewhere, we may not feel truly fulfilled upon our arrival; and or more importantly, we come to realize that the 'leaders' at the front have no clue where they're going, and the 'followers' just need someone to follow because they of course, are also lost.

How do you find your North Star, *your* true north? How do you find your path in life, and ultimately find your purpose?

It was 2007, and I just got out of the military after serving 5 years and 8 months (with an honorable discharge of course). I felt lost, alone, and had no real clue as to where I was going and truly felt mediocre. I felt like this for quite some time; maybe for 3 years at least, before I finally realized **I had to create my own map.** I created my own road map of where I wanted to go and had to dig deep to understand that I needed to essentially **'re-build' myself** mentally to bring this road map to life.

Of course, there were countless hurdles, obstacles, and walls that I perceived were there to keep me from going where I thought I needed and wanted to go. After much reflection, growth, and review, I now realize that those obstacles (often situations) were not there to keep me out, but to test my resolve, and to see how bad I truly wanted it. They made me fight harder, dig deeper, and more importantly, **think and believe differently**. To think at a different level and see from a different perspective, but also to believe and trust in myself at different levels of life that I find myself.

The Great Recession of 2008 was probably the largest obstacle.

"It's not what you get, it's who you become that is the prize..." ~anonymous.

As a die-hard sports fan, it took me 37 years before I realized that my beloved Atlanta Falcons could win the next 10 Super Bowls and it would not benefit me in any way, shape, or form. However, since childhood, every American is told or subconsciously shown to obsess over sports, music, television, entertainment etc.

Your favorite team could win the next 10 World Series...

Your favorite artist could win the next 10 Grammy's...

Your favorite actor/actress could win the next 10 Oscar/Emmy awards...

Your alumni could win the next 10 College championships...

The Game of Thrones could redo the ending 50x times picture perfectly...

How does any of this impact your quality of life in any aspect? Distractions.

How does this consistently put money in your bank account?

How does this improve your marriage?

How does this help get you the promotion or close the deal?

How does this help make you a better parent?

This book is not about my journey; it's about yours.

"The journey is the destination," ~ Dan Eldon.

Life Lesson 2:

Get Out of Your Head

"Drop the past, learn the lesson, & move the $#@! On…" Mel Robbins.

Your parent's story is their story. Their failures are their failures. Their success is their success. Their story has nothing to do with yours. Both of Michael Jordan's sons were horrible at basketball. They are not failures by any means, but basketball (AS A SKILL-SET) was simply not part of their story.

Your parents are not Superman or Wonder Woman. They're Clark Kent and Diana...
They're human, and they screw up just as you do…
They have made mistakes, and they will make mistakes…
They have errored just as many times as you have, if not more...
That doesn't make them bad or evil people…

It doesn't make them a disappointment or a burden...

It makes them human.

They have a part to play in your story, a necessary part. Their role was to physically bring you into the world and raise you (and yes, I understand some folks didn't even get that). However, even that may not have been a curse, but a blessing in disguise...

A necessary struggle.

I encourage you to try and embrace your struggle; everyone can relate to it. Its why people cry at graduations, it was never about the course works, homework, or exams; it was about the struggle. **It was or is about your journey** that helped groom **you into who you needed to be.** I encourage you to try and find some purpose to your pain. This has always been what we truly love about some of our favorite characters in the entertainment or sports industry:

Rocky (Movie) - Sylvester Stallone
Juicy (song) – Notorious B.I.G.
Game of Thrones (tv series)
  - Jon Snow
NCAA's Sweet 16 Basketball
  Tournament
Don't Stop Believing (song)
  - Journey

The Olympics
Rudy (movie)
*Any Disney movie ever

Their journey, their struggle, helps remind us of how we can conquer our own. It's a never-ending reminder of how we can be the hero of our own story. Simply put, there's **power in your struggle**, and that's a powerful way we all connect at the human level.

"Just because something doesn't do what you planned it to, doesn't mean it's useless," Thomas Edison.

For those who were raised without parents (death aside), would you have ended up just like them? The case in point – an alcoholic mother, drug addiction, just a bad parent, or a bad example of a husband or wife, etc.

It hurts, but one lesson learned is that **you have to love some people from a distance**, and that everyone has a necessary lesson they have to teach you. It has been said that people are in our lives for reasons and seasons. Meaning that they will not be around forever, but that we are all here to help teach each other a necessary life lesson, even the painful ones.

You do not get in life whom you want, but whom you need…

[to help you grow you into the person you've become].

"He had to release his history, to reach his destiny," TD Jakes.

Life Lesson 3

The Necessary Struggle:

"Wounds Are Where the Light Enters," -anonymous.

Your struggle is there for a reason, to teach you something and also note that suffering can often be seen as a mental habit. Your situation or circumstance is not a life sentence.

Understand, acknowledge, and accept the fact that where you are and who you have been and always will be, entirely depends on you. You cannot blame another human being, entity, government, or situation for where you are and who you are.

"You don't see the world as it is, you see the world as *you* are..." -anonymous.

They say the greatest day of your life is the day you were born and the day you figure out why; but to add to this, the day you understand and make sense of the 'worst day of your life' will absolutely be a life-changing moment for you.

The car accident, your parents' divorce, you failed in school, you got fired, etc....

What was the real and **necessary** life lesson you were destined to learn? Who did you happen to meet because of the situation or circumstance that you wouldn't have met, had it not happened?

In addition, what if your 'sad story' isn't sad at all? True, it may not be going the way you deem it to go, but *what if* there is something in it for you to develop and learn from? The college athlete who didn't make the league? The actor who never made it big? The hopeful medical student who never got into medical school. Your sad story, may not be a sad story, **what if you were just telling your story wrong?**

What if there was a different path for you, and you're simply not at a level in your life where you can understand it? The tortoise and the giraffe may see the same thing, but their perspectives are completely different and as a result, neither is right or wrong; it's simply their perspective in play.

The struggle is a part of your story.

The Necessary Struggle:

I was once standing outside, and there was extremely heavy rainfall. It seemed like a mini-hurricane with wind and thunder. I remember thinking, "Damn, this sucks. I hate it when it rains." It just so happened that I was standing next to a young dude who replied, "Man, it's just God cleaning the Earth."

This was a powerful moment for me as what he did was help change *my perspective*. It wasn't that he was right or that I was wrong; it was just a matter of a place and time that someone allowed me to see from a different perspective.

Sometimes we aren't given what we want in life because we simply are not disciplined, developed, and mature enough to handle it. Understand, acknowledge, and accept the fact that where you are and who you are, what you have been, and always will be, entirely on you. You cannot blame another human being, entity, situation or circumstance for where you are and who you are.

*"Step out of the history that is holding you back. Step into the new story **you** are willing to create,"* -Oprah Winfrey.

You have zero control over where you start in life, and we can say that maybe 80% of your start is on whoever raised you (including your 'community', extended family, friends, neighbors, school, etc.) But you have to come to grips with the fact that since you've graduated high school and turned 18,you are, by all means, a legal adult and **where you are and who you are, totally depends on you.**

> You make the decision to go the extra mile.
>
> You make the decision to 'Netflix & Chill'.
>
> You make the decision to read 1 chapter a day.
>
> You make the decision to start the business.
>
> You make the decision to write the book (or to finish it).
>
> You make the decision to stay up until 2 AM and party.
>
> You make the decision to go to Barnes-n-Noble over the club.
>
> You make the decision to spend your money at the mall.
>
> You make the decision to invest your money on businesses that actually own the mall(s) you shop in (google – 'Simon Property Group').

It's not the situation or circumstance that you were born in that defines you, it is your response to that situation. It is your response or decision on how to respond to that circumstance that do.

The Necessary Struggle:

If you get a flat tire, are you going to leave the car on the side of the road?

If the engine in your car fails, do you decide to pay to get it fixed or leave it where it is?

While I can certainly understand and accept that many (if not millions) of people are more than capable, hard-working, and willing to try; but are overwhelmingly limited to access of resources, i.e. well-funded schools, transportation (to and from) a school or gainful employment, or even a safe home. What I am focused on are the ones who 'can' but 'didn't', more or less because they do not see the 'how'. What I'm referring to is *a lack of vision for your own life.* Those of us who failed to realize that we can change everything with a choice, decision, and true perception, of who we are and where we are in the world.

You struggle with your struggle.
Your struggle makes you strong.
If you get caught up in that struggle, you lose the lesson.
The struggle was a lesson. It was necessary to teach you, to grow you, because it's strengthening something in you that's weak.
You have to build yourself up to benching 250 lbs.
That struggle is there to make you strong, to push you, not to pull you down.
If you miss the point of your struggle, you miss a key lesson life taught you.

The struggle is necessary.
The struggle is necessary.
The struggle is necessary.

You may be looking at it wrong (it may not be a struggle at all). Suffering is in the perception of the facts, and struggle is just a part of your story.

Your belief system:

"We all have a story we tell ourselves about ourselves," Lisa Marie Jenkins.

Where you are and who you are is largely determined by your belief system. I once attended a conference, and the gentleman asked, "why do you dress the way you dress? Why do you drive the car you drive, live where you live etc.?"

You have been selling or telling yourself (and others) this story, this belief system over and over; often this can be either a good story or a self-perceived 'bad story', but it's a story we repeat over and over to justify our behaviors, habits, and ultimately, to craft our identity.

"My parents were poor"	"I just went to a community college"
"I come from the projects"	"I was raised to believe…"
"I'm a 'minority' in America"	"Formal education is the only way"

The Necessary Struggle:

"I was born…"	"I need an MBA to make money"
"I failed in school…"	"They were born lucky…"
"I'm not a good reader…"	"Their parents gave them that"
"I didn't go to private school"	"I wasn't trained to do x,y,z"

Under the US Equality Act, there are nine protected characteristics:

- Age.
- Disability.
- Gender reassignment.
- Marriage and civil partnership.
- Pregnancy and maternity.
- Race.
- Religion or belief.
- Sex.

https://www.hrw.org/sitesearch/discrimination

I understand that we all have a sad story, but sometimes it's hard to tell if that is a story, an excuse, or just a justification for our failures.

How many times in your life have you been wrong? There are 365 days a year, and if you make three mistakes a day (small, medium, or large), that is over 1,000 mistakes a year. And since you are human, you're flawed by default, and it's by design. You have to make an error so that hopefully, you'll learn to correct it. What if how you've viewed your life is not 'wrong' per se, but *what if there's another way to look at your story?* A different perspective.

How or why you were brought into the world (your situation or circumstance)? What if there's a '**necessary lesson**' you were destined to learn? Sometimes your eyes only see what your mind is prepared to understand.

It has been said that we are exposed to things because we're supposed to do something about it.

The point is, you, me, 'we' are wrong quite frequently, and therefore, I can't help but wonder, *what if our belief system (this story we've been telling ourselves over and over and over) is simply wrong?*

Sometimes failing to get your 'goal' sets you up for your destiny.

Maybe you weren't rejected, but divinely redirected?

You have to come to grips with the concept that **your struggle is necessary.** We all go through a 'necessary struggle' (a rough patch) to help grow us, teach us, and build us to become a better version of ourselves.

When I first read the following quote, it really irritated me, because I knew it was right and that I had messed up:

"We're all self-made, only the successful will admit it," Earl Nightingale.

Everyone struggles at one point in life. They say half of Americans suffer from depression (focusing on the

The Necessary Struggle:

struggles of the past (yesterday, last month, last year, 10+ years ago, childhood)) and that the other half of Americans suffer from anxiety (anxiety is caused by stressing about events (future struggles and failures) that haven't even occurred yet).

"It never rains forever," anonymous.

Have you ever had that typical 'bad' 15-30 minutes where you woke up late, stubbed your toe, lost your keys, got stuck in traffic, and then you just decide to determine that the entire day is 'bad'? What you had was merely a 'bad' 15-45 minutes and you made a conscious decision to react and label the remaining 23 hours as 'bad'.

The 3 C's: What if there's a better way to do you?

Here's an example in which **you can directly control, change, and take action.**

Clothes (**small** example):

If you do not like the clothes that you are wearing, **could you, right now**, go to Macy's (or a consignment store) and select a new outfit? Something that can express this 'new you'?

Car (**medium** example):

If you do not like the car you are currently driving, **could you, right now**, go to a car dealer and purchase/

trade-in for another car (granted, let's do some homework and research on our numbers first)?

Career (**large** example):

If you do not like your current job or career, **could you, right now**, go to LinkedIn, Indeed, or Careerbuilder.com and search for your 'dream job'? Could you then identify ten people who are in that role, *study* their skill sets, education, certification, and experience and begin to **emulate their pattern**; so that you can replicate it to look like a more competent potential for your 'dream job'?

The point being is that **you could, right now**, do something and take legitimate action to change something small, medium, and large in your life. Regardless of your 'belief system' you can decide to take action to change your life. The 'terms and conditions' may not be ideal, but there are real steps that you can take to change your current circumstances.

What if we bought into a belief system that was not our own and came to find out, we could easily change it? The famous philosopher, Eckart Tolle states that:

> *"Whenever you're in a situation you have three choices:*
>
> **Change** *the situation.*
>
> **Leave** *the situation.*
>
> *or*
>
> **Accept** *the situation.*

But never complain, because when you complain, you become a victim, as if you have no power to choose to do something."

It is not about where we've been and where we're going, but about **who we're becoming in the process.**

You see, it's not that you can't; it's that you didn't. And once you decide that you will, my question is, *how will you?* I already know that you can, <u>*what's the plan to get from where you are to where you want to be*</u>?

Be specific.

What's the who, what, where, when, why, and how of your roadmap?
What's the who, what, where, when, why, and how of your life plan?

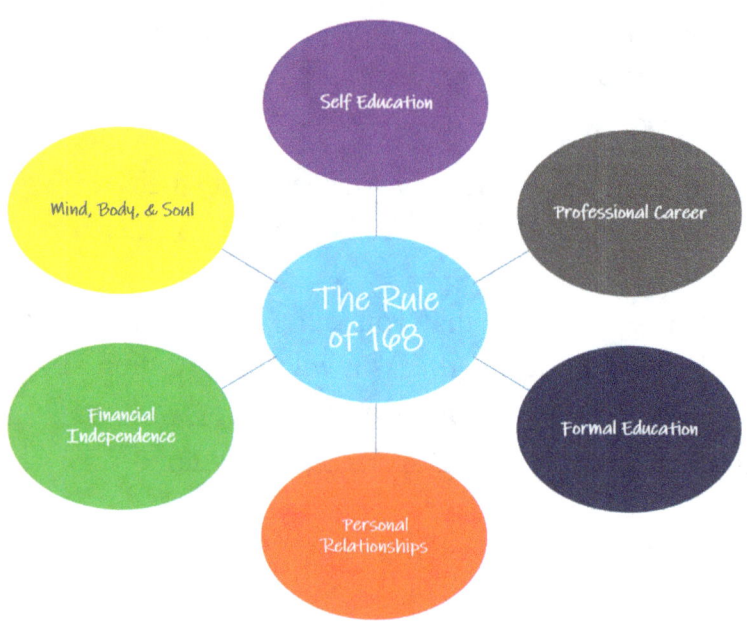

Fleas in a Jar:

One of the planet's greatest storytellers, Zig Ziglar, shares his best story of the 'fleas in a jar':

> *"You train fleas by putting them in a jar. You put the top of the jar and watch those fleas, and they'll jump up and hit the top over and over and over. You watch them jump. Finally, after they've been jumping a long time, you will notice that even though they continue to jump, all of sudden, they are no longer jumping high enough to hit the top. Then it's an absolute fact that you can take the top off the jar and they'll keep on jumping and jumping, but they cannot jump out.*

The Necessary Struggle:

You see, they have conditioned themselves to jump, just so high. And once they've conditioned themselves to jump just so high, that's all there is. There ain't no more. Man is wired the same way.

He starts out in life to climb the mountain, to write the book, to break the record, to do something with his life. But along the way he bumps his head, he stubs his toe and he becomes a SNIOP.

S.N.I.O.P.

[A person] Susceptible to the Negative Influence of Other People."

You have a homework assignment, as one smart person on the Internet declared:

" 1. Accept how you feel.
2. Know your purpose.
3. Do what needs to be done."

~anonymous.

Simply put, rebuild the belief system...
...and rebuild your life.

Life Lesson 4

The Ultimate Distraction

"Hood ni--a" by Gorilla Zoe

I was once in the flea market buying fake Jordan's with a friend of mine (because we couldn't afford the real ones), and a song came on while we were there. The song was, "Hood N---a" by Gorilla Zoe, a local Atlanta rapper. I jumped and said, "Whoa, I love this song! The beat is insane!"

He responded without hesitation, "I love this song because that's all I am, a hood ni--a." This cut me very deeply because it was at this moment when I truly understood the impact of influence. All at once, it came to me that **we are impacted** (either positively or negatively), by everything that we see and everything that we hear.

Every TV show either positively or negatively, has an impact of influence on us. Every song either positively or negatively, has an impact of influence on us.

Every 'celebrity' either positively or negatively, has an impact of influence on us.

Every family member either positively or negatively, has an impact of influence on us.

Every 'friend' either positively or negatively, has an impact of influence on us.

Every human being that we meet, see, read about, or hear about either positively or negatively, has an impact of influence on us.

Every situation or circumstance either positively or negatively, has an impact of influence on us.

In this instance, I realized that this 30-year-old intelligent man, this man who was brought into the world by a higher power, this man who had the ability to climb Mt. Everest, this man who had the ability to graduate from any university on the planet, or start a business, simply saw himself as a 'hood ni88@'. He had become distracted from his own greatness.

But how many of us have?

"People never outperform their own self-image," Tony Robbins.

We are distracted by the language that we use towards one another, the b-word, the h-word, ladies with makeup, hair - distracted from our inner beauty and/or **what we *perceive* as beauty** (usually based on what is trending this week). We are distracted by the current trends, fads, and of course, whatever is delegated as 'popular' by the masses.

We're distracted from our passion and purpose, always looking to get involved at some level, i.e. social media and 'cancel culture'. It's almost as if we need something to hate; something to distract us from the life we've built.

It almost feels as if we've been pre-programmed to waste a life. By the age of 2, my son had already learned how to watch Netflix and use the iPad; of course, it's what he's seen me do.

We've been distracted from our passion.
We've been distracted from our purpose.
We've been distracted from our dream.
We've been distracted from our own potential.

What are we distracted by? Our pre-programming (Mom, Dad, Grandparents, "my family", our community, etc.)

We've been pre-programmed to be distracted from living our best life.

Sold or distracted to do what other people tell you to do.

Go to college.
Get a career.
Get the car.
Get the house.
There are 40 hours in a week.
Spend 40 hours a week doing something that you get paid for and not working towards something that you love.

The Ultimate Distraction

Pre-programmed to be distracted by who, what, where, when, why, and how your life 'should' look. We live in a world that eats, sleeps, and prays at the feet of 'insert trending celebrity'.

They teach us how to walk, talk, dress, and carry ourselves.

✎ Pro Tip:

Don't take life advice from people who suck at life.

But it's Just Music

"Music is psychology. And if the music does not penetrate the heart, the soul, the mind, and the body, then you ain't gonna feel it. Because reggae music is not something you hear, it's something you feel. Ya, see? And if you don't feel it, you can't know it. It is a spiritual music with spiritual ingredients for spiritual purposes. The roots come from Africa, where all roots come from. It's a spiritual motivation of inspiration and through divine lines of Jah Rastafari. Who is the creator and always will be,"

~Peter Tosh.

By now we've established that whether or not we like to admit it, every person (celebrity), place, or thing either positively or negatively has an impact of influence on us.

An article published in 2003 in the Journal of Personality and Social Psychology, reported that "music could incite aggressive thoughts and feelings. During five experiments with 75 female and 70 male college students, those who heard a violent song were shown <u>to feel more hostile</u> than those who heard a nonviolent song from the same artist and style."

"Researchers at the University of Groningen showed in an experiment that listening to sad or happy music can not only put people in <u>a different mood</u> but can also change what people notice. In a 2011 study, 43 students listened to happy or sad music in the background as they were tasked with identifying happy and sad faces. When happy music was played participants spotted more happy faces and the opposite was true for sad music," Nina Avramova, CNN.

In America, we eat, sleep, and breathe with TV, music, movies, and pop culture in general. We have become so distracted (or even obsessed) with celebrities and the entertainment industry, that we seem to think that they are actual leaders in the community versus being mere entertainers who sing or dance. We eat in front of the TV, we check our phones before we get out of bed in the morning, and some of us even check our social media updates while we brush our teeth (I know…).

If we were to take a general glance at the quality of these programs, it speaks volumes. For example, three of the most popular shows in the country are: *Scandal, How to Get Away with Murder, and Breaking Bad.*

The very names are incriminating, but naming a show, '*How to Get Away With Murder*' is mind-blowing. Of course, Breaking Bad, one of the greatest shows of all time, featured 270 murders during its run. Scandal featured the main character having an affair with a married man. Have you ever known of someone to actually have an affair, the results are devastating, not sure why this is a prime source of consistent entertainment?

All three shows are largely about violence, sex, and drugs; a long walk from The Cosby Show, but of course now we know, even that was a lie (thanks a lot, Dr. Huxtable).

I'm not sure how we can have a positive life with a negative mind. In the well-known 'Rocky/Creed' boxing series, the infamous '**trumpet**' blows to begin the 'Eye of the Tiger,' and you can almost feel the *reaction* of *intensity* in the movie.

When you visit a spa, what type of 'music' do they play? 'Relaxing' spy music, and **the reaction is** you may fall asleep and/or fall into a relaxed state upon hearing the song. Even the atmosphere is different, and this is often due to the tone of the song.

When a baby is crying, what type of 'music' do they play? Lullabies and **the reaction are** babies tend to fall asleep upon hearing the song. Just type in 'lullabies' into YouTube and see the 100 million views that most parents may already have as a favorite channel.

When you attend any sports game, what type of 'music' do they play? Any song to get the adrenaline and energy pumping, so **the reaction is** the crowd responds with heightened energy and enthusiasm.

When you attend a funeral, what type of 'music' do they play? Amazing Grace and **the reaction are** attendees tend to sing, hum, and/or cry.

When you attend a wedding, what type of 'music' do they play? Most folks in 'Chocolate City' are familiar with the Stevie Wonder classic, "A Ribbon in the Sky'. Once played, **the reaction is** the crowd cries (and men pretend not to).

In a famous episode of the TV show, "The Fresh Prince of Bel-Air" the main character, Will, hugs his beloved 'Uncle Phil' when he finds out that his long-lost father abandoned him once more in one of the series most infamous episodes. Basketball phenomenon, LeBron James, admitted via Twitter, that upon seeing that episode, that he 'still cries...' (there's an emotional **reaction**).

I once had the pleasure of attending the Essence Music Festival in New Orleans (Essence is a "lifestyle magazine directed at upscale **African American** women"), and after attending the concert with a group of friends, we went to several after-parties on Bourbon Street. To my surprise, we entered one nightclub that was playing a particular song, "F-in' Problem," by hip-hop artist,

The Mediocre Miracle

A$AP Rocky. What was shocking to me was that, even at a concert and event that was specifically catered to 'upscale' women, the song, in general, was incredibly disrespectful to women. Check out the lyrics:

"I love bad bxxxxxx that's my fxxxxx' problem (Problem)

And yeah I like to f@ck I got a fxxxxx' problem (True)

I love bad bxxxxxx that's my fxxxxx' problem (Problem)

And yeah I like to f@ck I got a fxxxxx' problem (True)

I love bad bxxxxxx that's my fxxxxx' problem (Problem)

And yeah I like to f@ck I got a fxxxxx' problem (True)

If findin' somebody real is your fxxxxx' problem

Bring ya girls to the crib maybe we can solve it hey

Uh yeah ~~hx~~ *this the finale*

My pep talk turn into a pep rally

Say she's from the hood, but she live inside in the valley now

Vacate in Atlanta, then she going back to Cali mm

Got your girl on my line, world on my line

<u>The irony I xxxx 'em at the same damn time</u>

She eyein' me like a ni--a don't exist

The Ultimate Distraction

Girl, I know you want this xxxx!

Girl, I'm Kendrick Lamar mm

AKA Benz is to me is just a car mm

That mean your friends need to be up to par

***See my standards are pampered by threesomes tomorrow mm*

Kill 'em all dead bodies in the hallway

Don't get involved listen what the crystal ball say

Halle Berry, hallelujah

Holla back I'll do ya, beast!"

What was shocking to me was **their reaction** to the song. With each verse, the group of mostly women got more and more excited, rowdy, and loud (to be fair libations were involved); however, it was weird to watch **their reactions**. I couldn't quite understand how and why women, who had just attended a women's empowerment conference during the day were now cool with a song that was blatantly disrespectful to them. The song is full of words and lyrics, that had they been stated by a 'regular' dude on the street would be sure to get a guy rightfully cursed out; so why was **their reaction** different to this disrespectful song (or any particular music, show, or movie)?

My question to you is what type of music is on your phone? What was the first song you heard today and/or **what was your reaction** to this? How did it make you feel? What thoughts came about upon hearing this song?

What TV show or movie did you watch last night? What was **your reaction to this**? How did it make you feel? What thoughts came about upon watching this?

The American Academy of Family Physicians conducted a study that showed "an average American youth will witness 200,000 violent acts on TV before age 18" and it makes me wonder what **the children's reaction(s)** will be to witnessing these acts?

This, of course, is no different than the last conversation you had with a friend, family member, co-worker, etc. How did the conversation make you feel? How did it impact your mood? What was your reaction to the conversation? Again I ask, how can we have a positive life with a negative mind?

*"We are shaped by our thoughts; **we become what we think**,"* ~Buddha.

Life Lesson 5

The Mental Diet

"You need a new normal (for new results, new actions)," ~The Guru.

America can be a funny place with the constant goal of trying to look and feel a certain way. The latest fad diet is always trending from the South Beach diet to Keto diet. There are some days we count calories, while the others we count carbs. There's a never-ending focus on a physical diet.

Get in shape! Get in shape! Get in shape!

However, I can't help but notice that many of us **need a mental diet**. Why is this never the goal?

You can control your feelings (your energy), your views on your experiences (your perception or focus), and your patterns of behavior. The mental 'state' you're in determines what you do.

The Mediocre Miracle

Change your focus, change your physiology, change your results is what the experts say. America is a phenomenal place to build a family, a life, and a future, but has an extremely complicated past (and even present).

America has been an established country for 242 years, and yet we've only had 16 years of peace in our existence. We have a national addiction to television. We have a national addiction to sports i.e. high school football, college football, and pray weekly to the National Football League.

Our neighbors to the north point out our enormous food portions, and of course, it's sugary contents.

mediocre thoughts = mediocre actions
mediocre actions = mediocre identity/belief system
mediocre community = mediocre opportunity
mediocre $ = mediocre choices
mediocre life = mediocre legacy

I went on a mental diet, which turned into a lifestyle years ago upon leaving the military. I developed new thoughts, new actions, joined a new community, and as a result, my financial state, career, and life, have never been the same.

Therefore, I invite you to do the same.

There may be a time in your life where you do not like who you are or where you are and if so:

-I invite you to take the next *21 days to build a new habit.*

-I invite you to take the next *90 days to build a new lifestyle.*

They say it takes three months to change your life essentially.

And much like a diet, the strategy is not easy, but it is simple.

Who do you want to become? Who have you decided to become?

Write down the best version of yourself—your highest self.

Where will this new you 'go'?
And who do you need to become to get there?
Make sure each day you are working towards this new you that would make YOU proud.

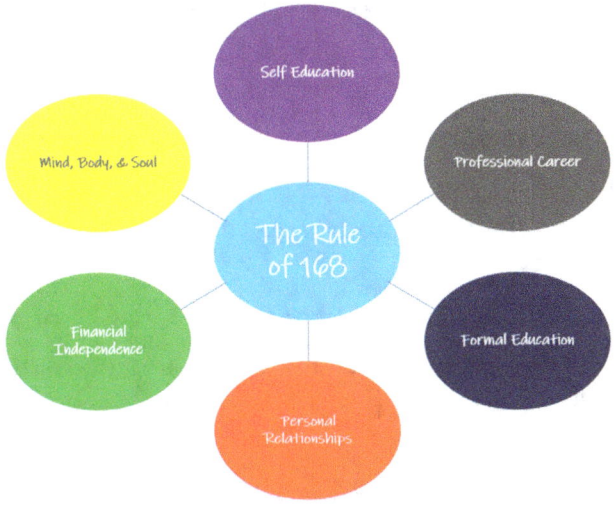

Life Lesson 6

The Rule of 168

"The Biggest Myth in America."

Go ask anyone in your family over 40 (and really of any age for that matter), how many work hours are in a week. The typical response, with no hesitation, is 40 hours. Most of us are taught that you work Monday-Friday, 9 AM- 5 PM, for a total of 40 hours a week. You can also 'prove' this by the nationwide stampede at 5 PM at most workplaces. People all over proclaim, "It's quitting time! It's Friday. The week is over!"

However, this is far from the truth. Let's do some simple math.

If there are 7 days in a week, and 24 hours in a day, 7 x 24 = 168.

There are actually 168 hours in a week, not 40 as we've heard over and over for years. So the myth is, on Friday, by 5 PM, that the week is indeed over.

The Rule of 168

It was about five years ago when I was introduced to a man by the name of Jim Rohn. Jim Rohn was a business philosopher who could take complicated business practices and translate them so that a child could comprehend. When I first heard the following quote, I knew that I had screwed up on a monumental scale.

> *"If you work hard on your job, you'll earn a living, if you work hard on yourself, you'll earn a fortune. Work harder on yourself than you do on your job,"*
> ~Jim Rohn.

I come from a hard-working, blue-collar family who insisted on a solid day's work, as remember, *everything* you do bears your signature. This was the attitude that I took into the workplace, work hard, work hard, work hard; however, once I was off the clock and the week was 'over', I would then begin what seemed 'normal' and begin watching television for easily 40-60 hours a week. I knew this was normal as I would go to work the next day and most of my coworkers (of various **ages, religions, races, and/or cultural backgrounds**) would discuss what shows they watched, the score of the game(s), and/or the latest movie released. By all means, watching television for 40-60 hours (or 6 hours a night) seemed right in line, so long as you 'worked hard' Monday - Friday, 9-5.

Therefore, when I initially heard the infamous Jim Rohn quote, *"If you work hard on your job, you'll earn a living, if you work hard on yourself, you'll earn a fortune."*

I knew that I was years behind. I knew instantly, that I had never worked on 'me' **outside** of the cubicle. This instilled a radical change for me in my thinking, behavior, and, ultimately time spent outside of work. As spending six years in the military, everything was laid out for me, how to dress, walk, talk, and what job to perform; therefore, upon leaving the military and this structure was taking away, I realized that I never put the equal amount of 'work' into my personal growth (be it emotional, spiritual, physical, mental, financial, relationships, aspect of my life, etc.)

We live in America, where the motto is 'Netflix and Chill", so implementing **the 'Rule of 168' is simple; you either spend a majority of your 168 hours both positively AND productively building a better life for yourself and your family or you don't.** There simply is no in-between.

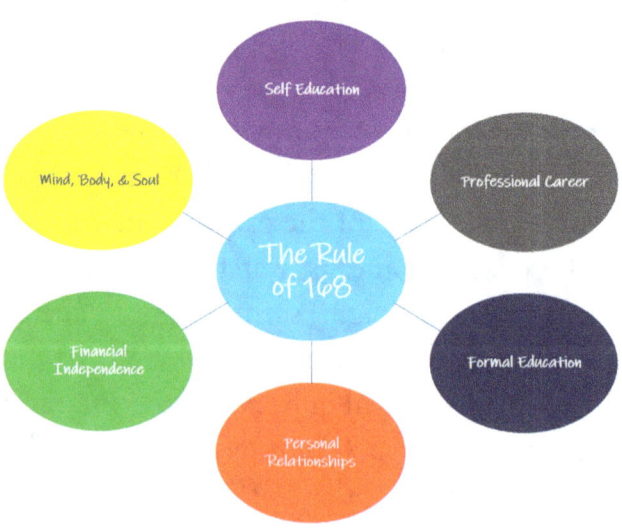

The Rule of 168

--40 hours on the job + 40+ hours on TV/phone + 50 hours sleeping.

--40 hours on the job + 40+ hours reading, family time, mental downtime (meditation), growth podcasts, community building, gym, + 50 hours sleeping.

Where do you spend your time?

A report by the New York Post showed that "a study by global tech company Asurion found that the average person struggles to go little more than 10 minutes without checking their phone. And of the 2,000 people surveyed, one in 10 check their phones on average once *every four minutes*. <u>*The average person checks their phone 88x in 1 day*</u>."

This is not a 'you' problem, but an *'anyone-under-30-problem'*, in that there will never be another point in your life where there will be enough time in your day; therefore, the best thing that I can say is to ensure that you're properly managing your time. In other words, you should always ask yourself the question – is what I'm doing right now, **positively and productivity impacting my life plan** (the plan **that I have decided** to create, live, & follow to improve my situation)?

You have to learn to perfect the 24 hr., as **progress equals happiness.**

Are you honestly progressing every day (not just Mon-Fri., 9-5)? I am sure you work hard on your job (part-time or full-time), but how many hours, days, weeks, and months do you honestly contribute to the growth and development of you **as a human, being?**

Are you right now, the best version of yourself?

If not, why? Can you honestly identify the distractions in your life? What do people see when you walk into the room (what do you want them to see)? What is your personal brand? How can you change this?

The point here is simple, in America, we teach you how to build a resume and not necessarily how to build a life. I'd like to challenge this premise.

Life Lesson 7

When the Student is Ready...

"Formal education will earn you a living; self-education will earn you a fortune. Work harder on yourself than you do on your job," -Jim Rohn.

Now that we've spent some time breaking down the importance of our thinking, our habits, and our 'belief' system, we need to make a transition; but this transition is quite a pivot because most Americans (and largely any citizens of any major country) focuses heavily on careers and of course, money. If you make the decision to live in America, you have to understand that you need to produce income to live, sustain, and survive in a country that is based on capitalism (meaning anything and everything is for sale). The dollar largely runs our country and most of all, if not all decisions are impacted by finances. Please note, I am not saying that this is right or wrong, but that it is just the way it is. My own goal is to secure a financial number so that the house, bills, and financial responsibilities are paid for or secured and that my family can focus on hearts rather than our wallets.

Unfortunately, many of us may reach a certain earning potential and 'declare' our lives successful simply based on a financial number as if earning six figures and going to the right school is a declaration on your life overall. I've lost count at the number of high earners I've met who are quite frankly, miserable, but because businesses and finances are such a central key of our culture, I would be remiss if I didn't cover this. As we are taught from kindergarten that our salary equals our level of success and is unfortunately why so many suffer from depression (often when we do not like the careers or life that we have built or chosen for ourselves and/or the money that comes with it).

As previously stated, I was in the military for six years; in addition, I came from a blue-collar family and went to public schools/universities that did not preach personal finance, entrepreneurship, and or wealth building. So, if you are like me, in no way is the 'system' set up to teach you how to become financially independent or business 'savvy'. So what do you do if your family, school, or you choose a career path that does not expose you to this concept of wealth creation to establish financial independence?

The real irony is many go to college to potentially *earn* a higher paying job, but colleges don't teach you *how to make money (or manage it)*. A bachelor's degree is when you take 40 classes on various topics. An MBA is an additional 12-20 class. However, I've met so many college-educated individuals who struggle with creating or knowing 'how-to' produce income consistently? Do you feel that colleges really break down 'how to' earn money? Most schools are tied to an ethical code that promotes theory over practical ways of generating income (which again, I am not declaring as right or wrong, but just as the reality). Have you ever heard of a major entitled, 'Millionaire 101'?

Do you truly understand how income is earned?

Simply put, you get paid to solve and manage problems and ultimately, how well '**valued**' your skill sets are to your current employer.

> *"You get paid for bringing value to the marketplace,"* Jim Rohn.

Mark Zuckerberg, Bill Gates, & Steve Jobs all dropped out of college and became billionaires (yes, I understand that these are the 'best and worst' examples); however, as we will elaborate in later chapters, they learned to solve problems on a larger scale, for billionaires, on a global scale. Who, how, and on what level do you manage and solve problems for people?

Remember, 'The Rule of 168':

> *"If you work hard on the job, you'll earn a living, if you work hard on yourself, you'll earn a fortune."* -Jim Rohn

Are you actively and consistently being positive and productive with your 168 hours? Be a student, in the area you want to improve in.

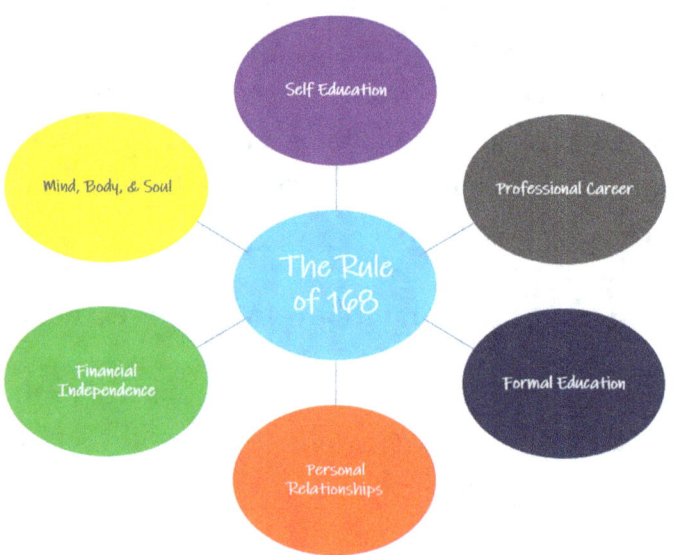

You want a million dollars via the lotto, but you do not possess the technical skill-sets to manage that money? We all would love a 6-figure salary, but could we properly manage the money? Do you have the self and formal education on financial independence to handle the money you'd like to have?

Famed college professor, Dr. Dennis Kimbro stated in his classic, 'The Wealth Choice, that "64% of lottery winners go broke as well as 84% of professional athletes" and you have to understand that these are regular human beings who came upon a large sum of money and were never trained or mentally prepared to manage it.

When the Student is Ready...

It's like wishing for a cruise ship or airplane and having no license, training, professional certification, or experience flying or sailing. Legitimate question here, but how many books have you read on personal finance? What if you read and or listened to one once a month for a year? Be a student; in the area you want to improve. If you'd like to earn more income, study those who earn more. Can we find the Bill Belichick of your profession, and emulate their success strategy? Can we find the happiest person you know and find out why they're happy? The same goes for finding a 'guru' in each area of our lives: Be it Financial, Career, Formal Education, Self Education, Personal Relationships, and especially for your own Mind, Body, and Soul.

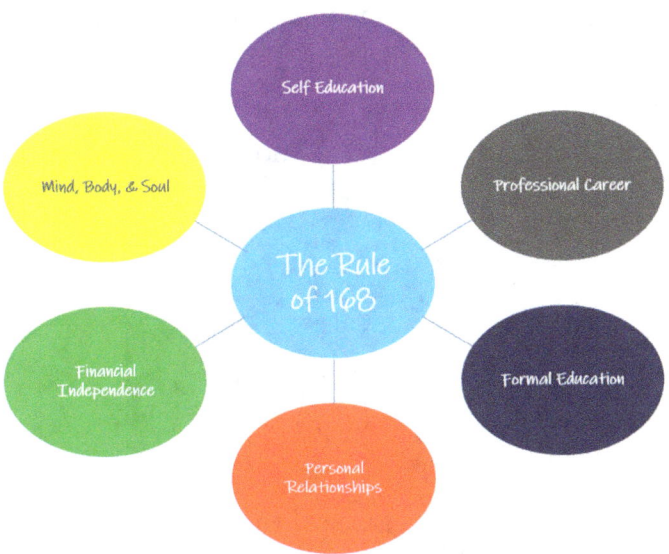

Point being, "*Work harder on yourself than you do on your job,*" Jim Rohn.

Life Lesson 8

Your Life Plan

There is a Japanese concept, "Ikigai" which points to finding your passion, purpose, what the world needs, what you can be paid for; essentially, your 'reason for being'. *Ikigai* is a Japanese concept that means "**a reason for being.**" The word translated to English roughly means "thing that you live for" or "the reason for which you wake up in the morning."

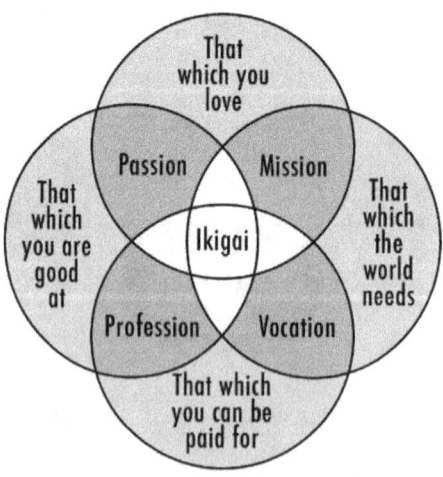

Time after time, I've heard someone in their 20's proclaim that they're going to go to college or grad school and shoot for a 6-figure salary with a Fortune 500 company. It is extremely fascinating to me that from kindergarten, we're taught to go to school, study hard, go to college, and start a great career as a doctor, lawyer, or engineer.

> School. College. Cubicle. Retire.

I hate to point out the obvious, but the goal is not six figures.

> Point being, *"most people don't lead their life, they accept it,"* -John Maxwell.

Upon leaving the military, it was a very hard transition for me, as no one gave me any marching orders, guidance, structure, or framework to follow to truly 'live', so how can you 'win' if no one shows you? I'd like to challenge you to legitimately think, pray, and meditate on what you **would love to have your life look like**. What do you feel is truly your reason for being? Not what you're currently being paid to do? I get irritated, and frustrated when I continuously hear and see so many folks so quick to resort to 'Netflix and Chill' when they've yet to figure this out yet.

Once you have the vision for that, then you can essentially make this 'road map' the most important obligation in your life? Going forward, let's break down what each area looks like and try to establish goals for where you want to go, as they will push you to become a better version of yourself to get there. But I also think it is important to point out that you will also need a role model, a coach, a mentor to guide you on this path you've chosen. In other words, if you are not a subject matter expert in one of the following, I'll pass on your opinion and/or I may follow your, example if I see that you are the example.

Quality of Life: Establishing Your Life Plan.

~Mind, Body, & Soul~   ~Self-Education~
~Financial Independence~   ~Personal Relationships~
~Professional Career~   ~Formal Education~

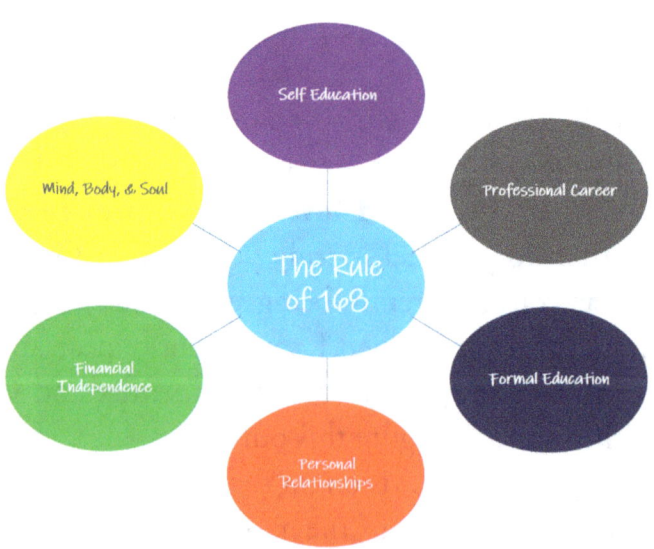

Mind, Body, & Soul

We will talk about business, your professional career, finance goals, etc., quite a bit throughout this book. Though I want to be extremely clear about one key point.

Finances do not equal fulfillment.
Finances do not equal fulfillment.
Finances do not equal fulfillment.

I've known several individuals who earn 6-figure incomes who sleep in separate bedrooms from their spouse(s). I've known depressed and alcoholic millionaires who died alone and brokenhearted.

~The Holes in Your Heart. ~

Money can and will bring a lot of opportunities to you, your family, and your future, but what it will not do is fill the holes in your heart. We have all been impacted and affected by a person, place(s), or event(s) that did significant enough damage to your being that it may feel as if there is a hole in your heart in that image. We often try and fill this hole with a temporary relief, alcohol, weed, cigarettes, sex, isolation, *binge anything* that appeals to us in that moment.

However, no amount of money, shoes, clothes, homes, cars, etc., can or will ever fill these holes. There is no amount of 'likes', retweets, or online followers that will help fill these holes.

From the time we're in kindergarten, we're taught to stay in school, study hard, go to college, select a career so that you can be happy with a 6-figure income. We've been *spoon-fed* the names, faces, and overall quality of life of our favorite celebrities who, largely via social media, share their beautiful homes, cars, and their overall *'happiness'* largely due to their incomes (or at least that's the pitch). However, if money is such an important piece of our happiness, how come so many people with money are, well, depressed? One of my largest issues with American culture is we put a heavy emphasis on educating our minds and not educating our hearts.

Your Life Plan

Anthony Bourdain
Robin Williams

Michael Jackson
Prince
Whitney Houston

Junior Seau
'The 27 Club' (Jimi Hendrix, Janice Joplin, Kurt Cobain)
Mac Miller
Kate Spade
*Brett Favre

All the above were millionaires, the best in their field(s), and/or idolized across the globe for having reached the pinnacle of 'success' and 'happiness'. Well, here lies the disturbing question – "why did one half commit suicide and the over half overdose on drugs or alcohol if they were so happy?" Let alone the number of military veterans who are estimated to commit suicide.

*It's worth noting, but Brett Favre did not commit suicide, but had a very public statement on his *addiction* to painkillers due to the injuries sustained during his 18-year career in the NFL.

If you asked me what my dream job was in my childhood, without hesitation, I would have told you to play in the NFL. As an adult, if you would ask me the same question, I would say to be 'partners in crime' with the legendary Anthony Bourdain. I simply couldn't think of another human being whom I thought had the best career (or life) overall? Mr. Bourdain was paid (extremely well) to travel across the globe, eat at the best restaurants, and drink the best beer. It seemed to be a global shock then when it was announced that he had taken his own life in 2018. How could someone with what seemed to be everyone's dream job, take his own life? This man was paid to travel, eat, and drink; and most importantly, it seemed that he was dearly loved by anyone who ever met him (and even by those of us that hadn't had the pleasure of meeting him in person).

Bonus question:

By now the entire planet has heard of Jeff Bezos and his e-commerce giant company, Amazon. Unfortunately, you probably saw Jeff Bezos had all of his personal business of his divorce and the alleged affair splashed all over headlines across the country. As it turns out, Mr. Bezos has four children who had to see their mother, father, and alleged mistress everywhere and I'm more than sure that every kid at school helped point out this embarrassing family misfortune. How are his kids holding up through all of this?

It truly makes me wonder, but *do you consider Jeff Bezos to be successful if he's a 'public success' and a private failure*? How many people do you know who deem themselves successful because of where they went to school, their career, and their salary, but are failing at home?

Yes, he's the wealthiest man on the planet, but if he comes home to an empty house and eats dinner by himself, is that truly the definition of a "successful life"? Do you think amount of Amazon stock, private yacht, or multiple mansions that he has can fill the hole(s) in his heart? It's also worth noting that I am not judging here, but simply observing his actions and the national reaction to this story.

It's almost American tradition that, come Friday at 5 pm to begin 'Happy Hour', party time or watches the game with a 'cold one'. We celebrate all occasions with food, music, and of course, alcohol. Alcohol and food are a large part of our American culture and traditions. However, one can't help but wonder, what is enough? Cigarette smokers, weed smokers, alcohol lovers, and food lovers can easily over-indulge and of course, find any reason to *consume*. One of the heaviest things I'd ever heard someone say was, "the question is not why the addiction, but **why the pain**?"
– Dr. Gabor Mate.

We were never trained or educated on how to *de-stress* from work, bills, or **life**. In certain parts of India, they teach their youngest students a class called, 'Life', in which they teach students simply how to breathe.

What is a win? What does 'success' really look like for you and your life? It's as interesting as in America, where we focus so much on money, money, money. We make songs about it, shout out to the O'Jays for the 70's classic, "For the Love of Money." For example, would you describe Pablo Escobar, Joaquin "*El Chapo*" Guzman, Floyd Mayweather, Jeff Bezos or the Menendez Bros. as 'successful'? My personal favorites are the endless Al Capone mugshots posted on countless Italian restaurants as if a notorious crime lord is something to aspire to be. Well, he made a lot of money, so does that justify all of his criminal behavior (insert sarcasm).

They are all millionaires, and several are even billionaires. It's fascinating that in America, 'success' is largely dictated on your bank account irrespective of how you obtained the money. Money is man-made and is not a true and totally accurate measurement of 'success'.

In 2002 when the famed mob boss, John Gotti passed away, he was given a full front-page memorial on the cover of the New York Daily News that stated, "The Last Don". It was almost a 'hero's' going away. For reference, "in 1992, **Gotti was convicted of five murders**, conspiracy to commit murder, racketeering, obstruction of justice, tax evasion, illegal gambling, extortion, and loansharking. He

was sentenced to life in prison without parole," according to court records and cnn.com This is the type of praise they give to an American hero, so why is a mob boss given such respect, honor, and praise? This is a horrible example because it clearly states that as long as you make money (legally or illegally), we will respect you. I hope to get half of that type of recognition upon my own passing.

It's never *health, knowledge, family, friends, community,* etc...but strictly monetary stature that seems to matter.

Pablo Escobar sold so many drugs in the 70-80s that he was listed in Forbes magazine seven years in a row as one of the richest men on the planet; and the same goes for Joaquin 'El Chapo' Guzman, the famed Mexican Cartel drug lord who escaped prison not once, but twice. What message does this send, not only to young kids but also to anyone by having these men featured in such an illustrious magazine as if 'they've made it' and they are the example to be?

Floyd 'Money' Mayweather has earned over $560,000,000 in the boxing ring and in his last two fights alone he earned over $200,000,000; yet his name never comes up with such 'People's Champions' as Muhammad Ali, Joe Louis or even George Foreman, all who took several loses while Floyd Mayweather went 50-0, an all-time boxing record. Ali is beloved because he stood for something much larger than income. Cultural **impact.**

It begs the question, **is it *income* or *impact* that we truly value as a culture?**

As previously mentioned, Jeff Bezos, the world's richest man, has gone through a very public divorce, and one can't help but wonder about the status and impact of this on his family. What of the Menendez Brothers, millionaire trustees who couldn't wait for their inherited fortune, estimated to be $8-$14 million, so instead, they took the lives of their own parents in 1989?

It truly begs the question, but what is 'success'? How do we measure it? It is said that the great Rev. Dr. Martin Luther King Jr never earned more than $10,000 per year, but there's not an American living who doesn't know his name. His impact on the world cannot be argued, but why was his income never brought into the discussion? We could say the same for Mother Theresa and Mahatma Gandhi in terms of the ***impact over income*** debate.

So what is successful, really?

We largely dictate that our careers equal our identity or that our salaries determine our success. Therefore, it means we must have been successful if we have earned a lot of money working for a large company; but it still remains a fact that no amount of money can cure your depression, anxiety, fill the holes in your heart, and essentially buy you 'peace of mind'.

What is success to you?

How many people can define success? Ask 1 million people, and you would get 1 million different answers. What does success look like to you and your life? How many people deem themselves successful because they hit a certain financial mark and even that is largely dependent on where you live. $50,000 is a lot of money to someone who lives in Mississippi, but $150,000 may have you living paycheck to paycheck in San Francisco or New York.

As a reminder, a fraction of the 7 billion on the planet lives off a $1 a day.

Some say they are successful because of where they went to college.

Some say they are successful because of where they live.

Some say they are successful because of what they drive.

Some say they are successful because of where they work.

Yes, you went to a great college, and yes, you make 6 figures, but if you are not impacting your very own community (meaning, **helping others grow**) are you truly successful?

In America, your identity is largely tied to your income or occupation.

I am a soldier.
I am a firefighter.
I am a lawyer.
I am a teacher.
I am a Googler (that's a real thing, by the way).

Is the kindergarten teacher who makes $40,000 a year who impacts 30 kids a day just as successful as the CEO of a Fortune 500 company?

I've never seen a U-Haul behind a hearse at a funeral, so you can't take it all with you.

Furthermore, it legitimately took me 37 years to figure this out, but our mental state of mind and our physical bodies are so tightly intertwined. It's why "a lot of people struggle with sleep because sleep requires peace," said some smart person on the Internet. **It is hard to be happy if you are never fulfilled.** In America, we never teach, praise, or value fulfillment as the end game to happiness; it's largely financial.

Your Life Plan

"Your life is your message," Eknath Easwaran.

Go tell someone in hospice how much money you make and see if they're impressed.

There is a phenomenal Brazilian story about a local fisherman by the legendary, Paulo Coehlo which goes as follows:

> *There was once a businessman who was sitting by the beach in a small Brazilian village.*
>
> *As he sat, he saw a Brazilian fisherman rowing a small boat towards the shore, having caught quite a few big fish.*
>
> *The businessman was impressed and asked the fisherman, "How long does it take you to catch so many fish?"*
>
> *The fisherman replied, "Oh, just a short while."*
>
> *"Then why don't you stay longer at sea and catch even more?" The businessman was astonished.*
>
> *"This is enough to feed my whole family," the fisherman said.*
>
> *The businessman then asked, "So, what do you do for the rest of the day?"*
>
> *The fisherman replied, "Well, I usually wake up early in the morning, go out to sea and catch a few fish, then go back and play with my kids. In the afternoon, I take a nap with my wife, and the evening comes, I join my buddies in the village for a drink — we play guitar, sing, and dance throughout the night."*

The businessman offered a suggestion to the fisherman. "I have a Ph.D. in **business management**. I could help you to become a more successful person. From now on, you should spend more time at sea and try to **catch as many fish as possible.** When you have saved enough money, you could buy a bigger boat and catch even more fish. Soon you will be able to afford to buy more boats, set up your own company, your own production plant for canned food and distribution network. By then, you will have moved out of this village and to Sao Paulo, where you can set up HQ to manage your other branches."

The fisherman continues, "And after that?"

The businessman laughs heartily, "After that, you can live like a king in your own house, and when the time is right, you can go public and float your shares in the Stock Exchange, and you will be rich."

The fisherman asks, "And after that?"

The businessman says, "After that, you can finally retire, you can move to a house by the fishing village, wake up early in the morning, catch a few fish, then return home to play with kids, have a nice afternoon nap with your wife, and when evening comes, you can join your buddies for a drink, play the guitar, sing and dance throughout the night!"

***The fisherman was puzzled, "**Isn't that what I am doing now**?"

The point here is **some of you will never be happy in the rat race.** I would like to challenge some of you to consider 'early retirement' now. How would you find your happiness as the fisherman has done in this story? Would you be open to a smaller home in another country where the cost of living is incredibly lower than in America? Belize, Kenya, or even India offer incredibly affordable lifestyles without the proverbial 'rat race'.

Do you need a $300k+ home in America, with a $50k SUV payment, a Louis Vuitton bag, Gucci sliders, and Chanel glasses to be happy? Amazon, Macy's, and every mall in America sell millions of items, but **they do not sell happiness.** Happiness is not something that happens on the outside but *within you*. It's also interesting how we try and pass on this belief of 'success' and 'happiness' to our children by trying to buy our children a happy childhood versus just providing them a happy home.

Mind, Body, & Soul: (BODY)

We even have to establish goals for ourselves physically, because as 'successful' as you may be with money, career, and material possessions, it's all pretty useless if your body is not in a position to literally carry you to where you want to go. Diabetes and heart disease are real factors and taking care of ourselves physically is one of the most important habits we can establish. What goals can we declare for ourselves in this area as well?

I once had a Chinese-Canadian friend who was visiting Atlanta, Ga ask, "Is it normal to eat fried chicken and sweet tea for breakfast?"

I remember being speechless, but offering a shoulder shrug as if to say, what else is there to eat? He was aghast at American food portion sizes and the amount of sugar and fat in our very processed foods as compared to Canada.

I was once fortunate enough to participate in two Half-Ironman triathlons in Augusta, Ga. In my first race in 2018 at Augusta, Ga, there was a contestant who was an eye-shocking 81 years old. Mind you, this race consists of a 1.2-mile swim (40-60 min.), 56-mile bike ride (3-4 hours) and half-marathon at 13.2 miles (2.5-4 hours) easily totaling over 8 hours of physical activity in one day, *non-stop*. I remember thinking this 81-year-old is probably just an anomaly and while he is incredible, I'll never see that again. The following year I saw a 77-year-old compete and finish as well.

It's worth noting that neither one of these gentlemen finished last :|

Mind, Body, & Soul - (Soul)

As we transition to 'soul', you have to understand that this will keep you grounded throughout the growth process, and it is honestly, probably the most important piece of the plan.

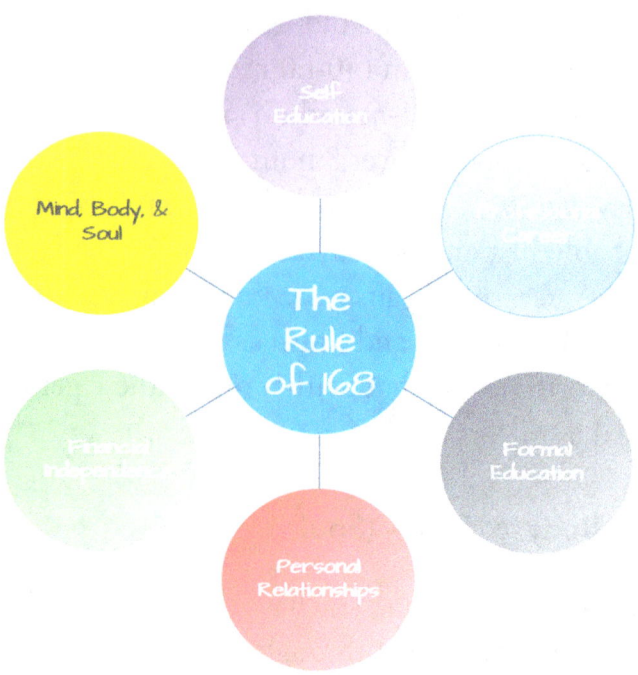

And allegedly, some of Steve Jobs' last words were, "At this moment, lying on the bed, sick and remembering all my life, I realize that all my recognition and wealth that I have is meaningless in the face of imminent death. You can hire someone to drive a car for you, make money for you – but ***you can not rent someone to carry the disease for you.***"

How much time do you spend by yourself? How much time do you dedicate to just breathing? We become so distracted by work, career, money, school, family, finances, and stress that we often just forget to breathe? How can we establish a time to breathe, but also to live? I ask that you, please make time to breathe, soul search, and prioritize 'you' time (this means no television or social media :|). It's hard to soul search and become grounded when you're constantly distracted by what is trending and more ironically, '**you**' are never trending and even if you are, it's usually not for the right reason(s).

You have to learn to breathe on your own, without fear, weed, alcohol, your parents, or any other human being impacting your breath because they say that your breath is the sound of your soul.

Keep breathing…
Keep breathing…
Keep breathing…

Financial Independence:

> "Do not educate your children to be rich. Educate them to be happy. – So when they grow up, they will know *the value of things*, not the price," ~anonymous.

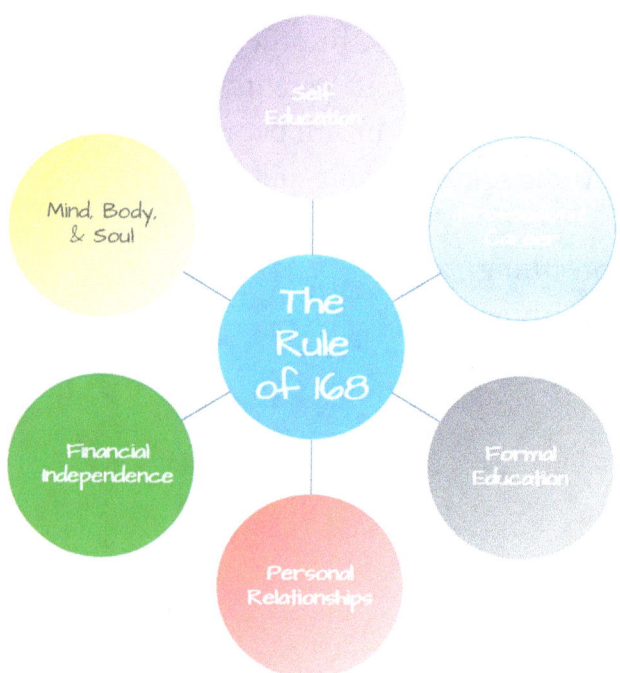

We learn about money largely from those who raised us. If our parents were spenders, we're spenders. If our parents are frugal, we tend to be frugal, and of course, our parent's example can be the ultimate idea of what not to do. The key here though is that financial education is not taught in schools, which is incredibly odd considering we're told from day one to study, study, study and prepare for the workforce to ultimately earn income; so we'll attempt to earn 6 figures, but at no point in time have we been formally trained or educated to manage this kind of salary.

Do you have a financial independence number? The exact number you need to no longer work for the rest of your life. The number to pay off the house, the bills, kid's college, groceries, etc.?

We cannot hit a target we do not have.

Would you like to own a house? How much would you like to invest in the stock market? Perhaps you'd like to own rental property? Pay your way through school? How much money *will you decide to have* in the bank in the next 24, 36, 48 months? How much money will you decide to make annually? How much money **will you decide** to be worth at the age of 50?

There's an Atlanta rapper, 'Young Dro', who boasted that he spent **$1,000,000** on his Ralph Lauren clothes collection (just let that sink in for a second). I can't help but wonder what would have happened had he invested that $1 million in Ralph Lauren's stock, perhaps? Do you think he had the financial awareness to invest any of that money into something as simple as an investment i.e., business (Subway franchise restaurant), rental property, or even a local school?

I ran the numbers, and though I doubt its authenticity, I took him at his word and assumed he legitimately spent $1 million on, unbelievably, *just* his clothing collection. Per his 'Wikipedia', he was born in 1979, and for argument's sake, let's say he invested that $1 million by 1999 (at the age of 20) into 'Ralph Lauren's' stock. Do you know how much that would be worth today? **$2,351,836.30**. I do not mean to make fun of, disrespect, or belittle this individual, but I do see a huge learning opportunity here. Clothes wear out after a few months; an investment of your money can last generations to come.

If you need proof, then you should take 30 seconds to google Antoine Walker, former NBA All-Star. This gentleman earned $110,000,000 in 12 years. After 24 months out of the NBA, Mr. Walker declared bankruptcy. If you do the math, he essentially spent **~$1,000,000 a month for an entire decade** (insert any emoji face you deem necessary).

As previously stated, you play the lotto to hit a million, but don't have the 'technical skillset' to manage it? Most people can barely manage their 40-50k salary, how then will you manage 40-50 million? Oddly enough, you'll more than likely have to hire a tax accountant, financial advisor, and a third party to ensure the first two hires will not cheat you and more than likely need a 4th hire to ensure that the previous 'inspector' wasn't cheating.

Go ask any of the potentially 37,000 people in 136 countries who were cheated by Bernie Maddoff (creator of one of the largest Ponzi Schemes in history).

My main point here is you need to establish goals for your own **Financial Independence** (and again, your 'life goal' isn't 6 figures, and in the event that it is, there is a difference between 'grossing' 6 figures and 'netting' 6 figures). Again, I ask, how much money ***will you decide to have*** in the bank in the next 24, 36, 48 months? How much money will you decide to make annually? How much money will you decide to be worth by the age of 50, not for material possession, but for financial independence?

It's odd that everyone wants money, but never studies it.

Famed financial advisor, Suze Orman states that "your net worth is largely predicated on your **self-worth**. It's why you swipe the credit card."

You make money but spend it all.

In 2002 when I was 19 years old, the military sent me to Afghanistan for a 6-month deployment during the war and upon my return, I had a whopping, $12,000 in the bank (that is an insane amount of money for any teenager). I put down $2,500 on my first car, a Dodge Intrepid (insert dance) and the rest of the money went, to bars, clubs, every clothing/shoe store in the nearest mall, you name it.

The Mediocre Miracle

I was broke in 90 days.

Had someone whispered in my ear to invest just $1,000 into the stock market with a company called Apple, today I would have $302,408.64

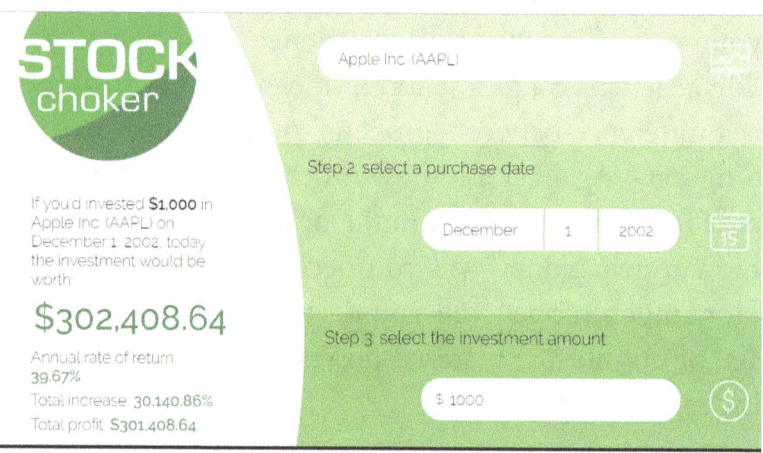

To be fair, someone may have told me this, but being 19 is extremely tough as we all seem to suffer from that feeling of 'knowing absolutely everything and absolutely nothing at the exact same time'.

In my six years in the military, I had never read a book on business or personal finance (this is my own fault and no one else's), so I essentially wanted things (more money) that I wasn't ready to handle. If you gave me $1 million, I would've spent the whole $1 million because in my own ignorant logic, I was never taught, "in a *formal classroom*," how to manage $1 million.

This is also important to declare, but the good news is had I had that $300k now, I would've probably spent it as well, so to be true, **I wasn't ready** for that type of money. Knowing what I know now, I would start a non-profit, invest in rental property, buy into a franchise, donate that money to my favorite cause, and or ensure someone else's life troubles are a little less cumbersome (and then buy a Lamborghini, I never said I was perfect).

Financial independence is important to establish economic safety for your family, your future, and not just to purchase the latest trend, as there is a big difference between being human and **human, being.**

You have the ability to impact and help so many people, I dare you to.

Self-Education:

I challenge you to be the valedictorian of your personal growth and self-education. My earning potential soared once I made the **mental adjustment that I was a business professional first and foremost** and that I could not solve business problems that I did not understand. I made an honest and conscious effort to become the valedictorian of my profession.

You either own a business or work for one.

How many (business) books do you (or could you) read in a month or year?

For reference, Bill Gates has claimed to read 1 book a week since he was 18 (I know…), and Warren Buffett reads "500 pages a day. That knowledge adds up like compound interest," he declares.

There's a website, https://willyoulaugh.com/books-written-billionaires/ in which there are 171 books written by billionaires. A book is largely when the author had an experience, a journey, or problem and **then wrote about the solution to such**. You could essentially read 171 books about how to start an empire to solve the next global problem.

Tim Ferris, brilliantly marketed as 'The World's Greatest Student' keeps an impressive list of recommended books: http://fourhourbook.club/ I love Tim because he does not focus solely on money, money, money. His list has an incredible range of topics, which, much like this book, focus on a larger picture for life versus just your annual income.

How many entrepreneurial seminars and or business conferences have you (or could you) attend this month or year? For clarity, it's not necessarily about who's on the stage, but **who's in the audience** (or specifically *who you're sitting next to*) that matters. Everyone there is someone motivated enough to spend time and money to invest a few hours into learning about something that could positively and productively impact their lives or business, why not exchange contact information and network with these individuals? This is another opportunity to sell you, your skillset(s), and your experience; and *show how you can help impact someone's business.*

As previously stated, you must come to grips with the fact that since you've graduated high school and turned 18 that you are, by all means, a legal adult and **where you are and who you are, is on you.** We cannot continue to blame our family, parents, school (formal education), government, our employer for our life, or level of education or information.

How many colleges now have courses or majors entitled, "entrepreneurship", "personal finance", how to make or manage a million, etc.? Unfortunately, some people think that their educational growth is strictly confined to what they can learn in a 'formal classroom' only (of course, I am referring to myself). But that formal classroom is designed by a man/woman and **cannot teach you everything** you need to learn in life; and nor, are they solely responsible for your level of education.

It is imperative that we establish goals for ourselves in the form of 'self-education'. If no one showed us, cool. How can we learn and be self-taught? There is simply too much information and resources out there for that to be an excuse.

Self-Education Goals:

Can we attend four business seminars a year?

Can we read or listen to something that will improve our lives in some aspect?

How can we use self-education to positively and productively improve our life?

Amazon Prime now has a show entitled, "An Entire MBA in 1 Course," so yes, you can go through an MBA program on television.

#TeamNoExcuses

Personal Relationships

This entire book could essentially be about relationships. There are so many types of relationships:

- -- Your relationship to the High Power
- -- Family relationships
- -- Your significant other
- -- Financial relationships
- -- Friendships
- -- Your relationship to your community
- -- Professional network
- -- Co-workers

I once had a co-worker in the military who was constantly moody, irritated, and frustrating to deal with. What we didn't know was that he just got divorced and not only had his relationship with his spouse impacted his work performance, but he was also denied a promotion, i.e. his annual raise.

How many times have you been to a restaurant and the waiter or waitress has an attitude and clearly didn't want to be there, and you may even see them 'angry texting' what appears to be a boyfriend/girlfriend and is usually a relationship issue?

This is called bringing *your mess to the workplace.*

When you bring your mess to the marketplace, it impacts your mind, body, and soul, your relationships with the people around you, but especially your money.

I am by no means a relationship expert, but a hard life lesson learned is how valuable relationships are as I try to live by two relationships 'goals':

1. "Stay close to people who feel like sunlight" -anonymous.
2. Try and understand people as essentially **everyone believes they are the hero of their story**, even the villains.

Famed Atlanta Pastor, Bishop Dale C. Bronner stated it magnificently with:

"The 7 Things Everybody Needs:

1. Everyone needs love.

2. Everyone needs a purpose.
3. Everyone wants to be somebody.
4. Everyone needs encouragement.
5. Everyone has something unique to offer.
6. Everyone can become more.
7. God uses people to help people."

You should never think you don't have an impact, as the relationship you have with people cannot be wiped away. *You have made an impact on their* **head**, **heart**, and, more than likely, their **spirit**. It was a phrase that says, "people are in your life for reasons or seasons," meaning that someone will not always be in your life physically, but that the message or lesson they've been put here to bring you (or teach you), will stay within you forever; their message, love, and love language has made an impact on your mind, body, & soul.

My own hope is that my family and friends remember my heart over everything else.

Personal Relationships: (Professional)

How many networking events can you attend in the next 6-12 months? Could you get 100 business cards in 1 year? Could those relationships help you close 100 business deals through these new relationships that'll impact your community in some way? Who will you meet that'll help you define your brand? Everyone you meet knows at least one thing you don't. Do you speak to people who are where you want to be daily or weekly (you need allies)? Ask them to take a look at your life plan once it's complete; it'll let him know you're serious, because people will not take you seriously if you don't even take yourself seriously. If your relationship builds, they'll be inclined to want to help you complete it.

Do you notice the difference between multiple sports champions and athletes who've never won or not won as many championships, i.e. Michael Jordan vs. LeBron James? You have to be surrounded by champions, hall of famers, people who will push you and pull you into a better you.

Every person I've ever met on this planet, whether they're white, black, Asian, Hispanic, gay/straight, Muslim, Jewish, or Christian, is going through some type of struggle. There are physical struggles, mental struggles, emotional struggles, spiritual struggles, and never-ending financial struggles.

"Struggle is a part of the story."

Perhaps the late philosopher Plato said it best with, "Be kind, for **everyone you meet** is fighting an internal battle." I think we often focus too much on the negative impacts of a struggle, our skin color, career placement, or religion, but rarely do we admit that the struggle is a good thing, for **the struggle makes us who we are.** The struggle is just as much as part of the story as the positive impacts it has on us. One of the hardest lessons learned is I now understand that **those hardest to love need it the most.**

Everyone needs a relationship, even the complicated ones.

I wish every high school and college in America had mandatory classes simply entitled, 'Family 101' with topics like *'how to be a better son, daughter, husband, wife, brother, sister, niece, nephew, spouse, parent, etc.'*

It should be mandatory that you should at least 'minor' in Family 101 as we all come from family and or many hope to establish their own someday. So how did we learn to be a spouse or parent, on our own accord of course? This may disappoint some, but we will either become just like our parents or make a conscious decision to be their polar opposites in style when we establish our own path in life.

<u>Furthermore, I've noticed that the three hardest things for someone to say are:</u>

- I love you.
- I apologize (as in, **I was wrong**).
- I need help.

As these three are largely deemed, 'signs of weakness,' and we are mostly *taught*, not to be weak. Some say that real education begins when we unlearn all that we were taught.

Again, I do not deem myself a relationship expert, as I am largely an introvert, but a few 'relationship' tips I've noticed:

1. "You date at the level of your self-esteem," said some smart person on the Internet.
2. Nothing good happens after midnight, (:|), be careful who you go home with.
3. Never lay down with a loser. If the person you're dating doesn't have long-term potential, please do not waste your time or theirs.

Relationship Goals with your significant other:

(Some) men make love with their 'points to manhood,' and women tend to make love with their hearts. I've been married faithfully for 15 years and I hesitate to give out relationship advice as I've certainly struggled here; however, there are a few key concepts I can't help but notice we all deal with. We bring our relationships struggles into work or may walk around with a broken heart, and it can impact any aspects of our lives.

"How we do anything is how we do everything," -anonymous.

* Be a student of marriage and learn how to become a great spouse.

* Study your partner. Study their wants, needs, and desires. One of the best ways is to ask a happy couple- what makes them successful. What are they doing differently? The key here is if you're the husband, don't ask the husband what he's doing, ask his wife. Only the opposite spouse can positively identify and, more importantly validate, what works for them; therefore, go to the source and vice versa for wives seeking to be better.

* Being a 'good' spouse can get you fired. People don't want just 'good', they expect 'great,' so don't be good.

* You're never *off* from being a spouse.

* They say it's a science to catch a man, and a full-time job to keep him (this of course, goes both ways).

* Build the friendship.

* They are 365 days in a year, you will make 365 mistakes, in fact gentlemen, you will make 720, sorry, those are just the rules, so establish a 'kindness competition' between the two of you.

* I've always noticed a trend, specifically with *married* women...

Some tend to talk down, 'joke', or insult their husbands (which is odd, because it consistently makes me wonder why they married him in the first place) and they tend to do this whether he is in the room or not. What I noticed is, if you talk down about someone, **you begin to see them in that manner.** Let me put this another way, if you talk about and see your spouse as the 'court jester' they will behave like the court jester, but if you talk them up (to friends & family) you will also see them in that manner, as a King (or Queen). If you talk to them, see them, and treat them as a King or Queen, they will have no choice, but to act or live up to that manner, and in response, they will begin to treat you as their Queen (or King). Again, this goes both ways...

Lastly, marriage has to be the 2nd priority (2nd only to God) but first to everything else, yes, even the kids.

The reason being, *you can't help someone if you're suffering*. When the airplane takes off, and the flight attendant gives the safety briefing, they tell you that in an emergency to put on ***your oxygen mask first*** – it's a priority. It's the same concept, take care of you, so that you can be in great position to take care of someone else. You will have a great career. You will earn a lot of money. You will have a great home. You will drive a great car. Yet, your spouse will care about none of this ***if you're not taking care of their heart, their love language.***

Every relationship needs 3 A's:

>Attention
>>Affection
>>>Appreciation

Personal Relationships: (Friendship)

"Your Vibe Attracts Your Tribe"

"Your net worth is largely predicated on your network," says anyone over 50.

By now, we've all heard of the infamous phrase, "birds of a feather, flock together".

*Weed heads hang around other weed heads.
*Athletes hang around other athletes.
*Religious folks hang around other religious folks.
*Police officers hang around other police officers.
*Doctors hang around other doctors.
*Military vets hang around other military vets.

Try and talk with those who make you see, feel, and love the world differently. What does your circle say about you? Who is in your 'crew?

"I don't have problems; I have friends," Clarence Avant.

Here's a great example, many people say that they want to earn an MBA, which is certainly understandable;

however, what they may have missed is what an MBA truly does for you. If you want to learn something, you can read, study, or research the topic; or you could learn about the desired topic via experience (actually applying the information). If you wanted to learn about business, why not start a business, just something small? Most people tend to apply for an MBA program, with the intention of 'learning about business, which again is fine, but the true added benefit of an MBA is who's sitting next to you in class. People attending MBA programs are most likely those seeking to climb the corporate ladder, entrepreneurs, or those who deem themselves as lifelong learners. These are most likely individuals who may be working for a Fortune 500 company one day, whom **you now have direct access to because a relationship was built** while you attended class together, "Hey, I went to school with 'x,' and he/she is now an '*executive*' at 'x' Fortune 500 company. Let me shoot him or her my resume." On more than one occasion, a friend has sent me their resume and if I felt that they were a good match, I would walk in *(with direct access)* to my company's HR department and place their resume directly in front of the HR Director and vouch for that individual. An MBA is a great way to grow your business skill set, but an even better way to grow your network. The online magazine, Business Insider, had a report that showed, " 70-80% of jobs received are through networking."

"It's not what you know; it's not who you know, **it's who knows you,**" Raymond Aaron.

What does your 'contact list' say about you? How many of your friends constantly tell you, "Hey, you have to read this book, it'll change your life," versus telling you about the newest TV, movie, celebrity, or album trending.

NBA All-Star Kevin Durant left the Oklahoma Thunder because he needed a change. He knew he needed to be around certified champions, not just really good basketball players. He knew that the Golden State Warriors would help *grow him* into a champion. He has since won 2 NBA Championships and was almost immediately catapulted into the upper echelons of All-Time NBA greats. And to think that just 24 months prior, he was labeled, "***Mr. Unreliable***" by the Daily Oklahoman newspaper. All that changed was his network.

"*Iron sharpens iron,*" Proverbs 27:17.

You attract what you are, what you are in sync with. They say that you're the average of the five closest people you're around. You compare and or influence each other's thoughts, ideas, beliefs, experiences, etc.

Who's the most 'successful' person you know, and why?

The best husband, the best wife, the best parent, the best athlete, the best at managing money, the best career professional, or simply, the happiest person? What if you were surrounded by this person 10 times a day? How much different would your life be if you learned from this person, specifically in the area of your life that you needed?

Lastly, I'll say one of the greatest pains I've noticed is when you may love someone and that love is not returned. You may love a potential signiciant other, girlfriend/boyfriend, friend, or even an in-law and your love may not be displayed or returned in the same respect; but a healed person may have love for you and never speak to you again.

I've learned that our love languages tend to be things we lacked as a children and sometimes you have to understand that there are certain folks who can only be in your heart, not in your life.

Relationships are such a crucial point of our lives and hold such a vital impact on our happiness, our head, and our heart. They say real wealth is not in the financial form, but in the form of relationships. I hope that your relationships help you grow into the person you are destined to become.

Formal Education

I understand that the need for formal education will be a never-ending debate for years to come. Do you need an MBA? Is it really that necessary for your path? How far should I go? Cost understandably may be one of the largest factors  as you can easily drop $100k on an Executive MBA alone. You could probably ask a million people and would receive a million different answers as to whether it is necessary or not.

Most missed the point, as it's not 100% solely about education, **it's about the discipline of finishing**, **time management, and being focused** enough on the 40 classes required, which in itself is a large *project*; as well as the networking ("Oh, I went to school with him. He's an HR manager at Dell. Let me shoot him my resume on LinkedIn").

In 2019 a huge story broke out labeled, "College Scandal: Operation Varsity Blues." In which some very famous 'celebrities' were caught essentially buying their children into some elite schools. Many people were shocked and appalled by this elaborate scheme, but I remember thinking, these people knew the significance of a 'prestigious network' and were essentially trying to **buy their way into that network.**

You see, you're the average of the five most people you spend the most time around and these parents knew this and were willing to risk prison time to put their kids in these networks. They knew these college networks come with billionaire alumni, future doctors and lawyers, future venture capitalists, and other talented and 'connected' individuals. I am not in any capacity justifying their actions, but I recognize their temptation to set up a better quality of life for their children.

You attract who you are.

Could you establish new goals to set the bar for your own family?

What would your graduation date be? Class of 20.xx?

Where will you go to school, and what will your major be?

When is the application deadline?

There are several key points that stand out for most of us now, though:
The sheer number of resources that are available to us now is astounding. You can attend college online,

listen to books vs. carry them, sit in on classes via web conferences, etc.

- Audible.com (for those who prefer to listen vs. reading material)
- Download course content onto your phone Attend courses online:
- Harvard University sponsors a school and program, Harvardx, in which you can attend Harvard, *'for the free free'*. https://www.edx.org/school/harvardx

I jokingly state that I have my Ph.D. from the 'University of YouTube' as the amount of educational and intellectual content on their site for free is phenomenal. Harvard College routinely posts many of its professor's lectures on the site.

There's probably no better ambassador for YouTube's content than Julius Yego, who is a Kenyan track and field athlete who competes in the javelin throw. "Nicknamed "Mr. YouTube" because he learned how to throw by watching YouTube videos of javelin athletes. Yego is the African record and Commonwealth record holder for the event with a personal best of 92.72 m," (Wikipedia.org).

While I understand the cost will always be an enormous factor, I can't help but think of the example being set not only for your kids but friends and family who may be inspired by your example to further your education as well. I never thought I'd be an advocate for formal education, as I often struggled with school growing up (primarily due to boredom), but once I found several subjects I was passionate about, i.e. business and technology, all I see are the benefits and opportunities that have come about as a result.

"Don't let schooling interfere with your education," - Mark Twain.

Professional Career:

I truly despise the heavy emphasis of career, career, career in our world, but again, we live in a time where your career largely impacts your finances and life overall. I cannot say this enough, but your career does not dictate your level of success or happiness. Your career is largely a chance for you to showcase your knowledge, skills, and abilities to hopefully impact your neighborhood and/or community. Therefore, we need to establish career goals, not for ourselves, but to further help and impact our communities.

In your full-time gig, how many promotions will you decide to get? If entrepreneurship is in your head or your heart, how soon could you start your business?

If you do not know how to start, could you find a local startup incubator to coach and teach you? Could you find the next career gig you want online (and dare to dream big, i.e. salary, benefits, etc.)? I challenge you to find three different business professionals on LinkedIn who are currently doing that job for a big company and compare their LinkedIn (skills/resume) to yours. Identify areas you need to work on to get that job you said you wanted.

As previously referenced, Dr. Dennis Kimbro, of the famed, Clark Atlanta Univ., wrote the classic, "The Wealth Choice" in which he profiled 250-1,000 black millionaires in the US, (so we know it's possible to build an empire) and yes, motivation is cool, but the heavy emphasis in the book was, they had a plan.

Your career is obviously incredibly important as you can carve out your own name, legacy, and impact on the world, however, if you've ever been to a funeral, **they will never read your resume at your funeral.**

My point here with all of this is to get you to focus all your thoughts, energy, and actions towards your life plan, not just your career, but your road-map, your true north; Again, this is not for selfish reasons, but so that you can be the example for the next person who needs an example of how to dream and ultimately, bring that dream to reality.

What's your plan? What's your plan? What's your plan?

Your life plan should include the following:
6, 12, 18, 36 months goals & don't be scared to pen down a 5 year and 10-year plan.

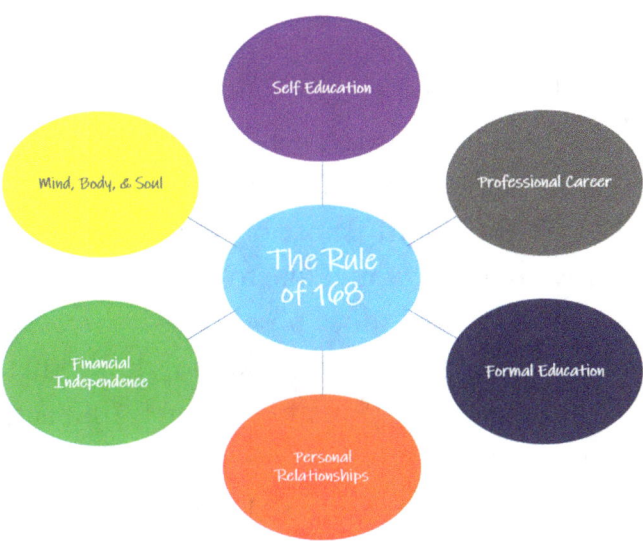

Life Lesson 9

But the Company Didn't...

Whether we want to admit it or not, working (and essentially our careers) is a large portion of our lives and, for some, may seem unfulfilling as I constantly hear, "what's the point," short of those who work in a monastery. Though I would like to point out that working, much like school, does pose *a bigger symbolic portion of our life*, as I would like to think that our 'contribution to society' may ultimately impact, improve, and enhance someone else's life. Therefore, we must make a conscious effort to understand and master business, because essentially, **anything and everything is a business**, or really a *business transaction*.

A business is built, established, and created to sell a product or service in direct exchange for money.

A business is essentially **a process**. That process is more important than any one person and is why each of us, me included, can be replaced at any time. I am not saying this is right or wrong, but that's just the way it is.

It's the way it has always been. It's what they mean by the statement, "it's just business, it's not personal." A business is like the seasons. We have fall, winter, spring, and summer and business is no different. There are good, bad, and ugly times in business, but quite often, even the 'perceived' bad times are necessary. They're necessary for re-growth, new ideas, new people, and fresh starts.

"Jobs are owned by the company, you own your career," Earl Nightingale.

A business is not built to make you a millionaire. It is like driving a car and expecting it to fly after it hits a certain speed. This may be a tough pill to swallow, but a job is largely meant to maintain you. The average American salary is $46k so it could be fair to say that they pay just enough for you to not quit, and in return 'we' often work just hard enough to not get fired.

I'm always shocked at the aunt, uncle, or grandparent who still holds resentment towards the company that closed or denied them the promotion or laid them off due to whatever circumstance at the time. You have to understand that by design, as a **business model**, a company (or more importantly, *our government*) are not built with the sole purpose to financially support you and your family; and even if they do it's the bare minimum amount (school financial aid, WIC, food stamps) for a short period of time, and it's typically during emergencies such as a recession, a war, or a government shutdown. You cannot expect, hope, trust, or bet on another human being, company, entity, or government to support you or your family, **long-term.**

NOTE: I'm not advocating for or against them, it's just the reality of our government's 'operating' model and largely how businesses are set up.

You need to understand:

There is no such thing as job security.
There is no such thing as job security.
There is no such thing as job security.

John Schnatter, the founder of the Fortune 500 company, Papa John's, was fired from the company **he started,** and they still use his name and face on the pizza box. And yes, he's a billionaire.

Antonio Brown, arguably the best wide receiver in the NFL, was fired from the best team in the NFL (2019).

Richard Nixon was in process to be impeached (essentially fired) as President of the United States but resigned before proceedings took place.

Steve Jobs was fired from Apple, the very company he co-created, fired him.

Walt Disney's newspaper editor told the aspiring cartoonist he wasn't creative enough.

Carly Fiorina, the first female executive of a Fortune 500 company, was fired as CEO of Hewlett-Packard.

The legendary Bill Belichick was kicked to the curb by the Cleveland Browns and has won 6 Superbowls with the New England Patriots since.

But the Company Didn't...

Abraham Lincoln was fired from his job as a captain in the army during the 1832 Black Hawk War and reduced to the rank of private.

Most recently, Adam Neumann, CEO, and founder of the startup, WeWork, stepped down from his company due to pressure from his investors.

The point here is if 'they' can fire a CEO, president, the best of his or her industry (**in their prime**) and/or founder of a company, they can fire, layoff, or eliminate you and your position. You may love your job, but your job may not love you back. Statistically speaking, you will be between jobs an average of 3x in your career either by choice or by circumstance.

There is no such thing as job security.
There is no such thing as job security.
There is no such thing as job security.

Please feel free to ask any of the employees of the following companies:

- Toys-R-US
- Forever 21
- Blockbuster
- Coal Miners
- Amazon's 'cashier-less stores'

Payless
Charming Charlie's
Sears
JCPenney's
K-Mart (used to be Wal-mart of the 60s-80s)

Even if you are the lucky ones, who have a certain guarantee of job security or pension, then there is the issue that the job is largely meant to maintain you, and not become you.

You are not your occupation.

I am an electrician.
I am a nurse.
I am a soldier.
I am an IT engineer.
I am a doctor.
I am a soldier.

These are not what you are; it's what you 'do'.

From K-12, college, the cubicle is almost preparing you for the workforce. There's a heavy emphasis in America to build a resume and not build a life.

Everyone works, works, works, and works.

It almost seems as if no one's satisfied because of no one is actually living, everyone seem to be working.

And we take this same mentality and pass it down to our kids and expect them to be just as unfilled as long as you are *financially compensated.*

The point is, just because our past generations worked for years and years, that doesn't make it right. It does not make it justified.

Were they happy?
Were they fulfilled?

What could you learn from this?
Were they living in their purpose?

Here's a legitimate question, but why do you get up and go to work every day? Besides paying the bills? Are you doing that because everyone else is? That's all you know, that's all you've seen our family and friends do.

And even then, there's the never-ending argument of an often self justified compensation.

"This job is on some bull$hit. They don't pay no money." is what I was told by a 21-year-old Georgia State senior who was interning with our company. She was crabby, irritated, and frustrated with her lack of pay at the company.

OK, I'll bite...

Me: "You mean, this job doesn't pay *you* any money. There are numerous people here who make over figures."

Remember, *"you get paid for bringing value to the marketplace,"* -Jim Rohn.

You get paid to manage and solve problems. If you're not solving problems deemed '**valuable**' by your current company, they simply won't pay as much, as that problem may not be that much of a priority to that specific company.

Here's a great example:

The Mediocre Miracle

Michael Jordan is largely considered the greatest basketball player of all time (though this particular LeBron James fan has a strong argument for another day), and there was a time where Michael Jordan was paid over $36 million dollars for one year of basketball (82 games). However, in the middle of his career, Michael Jordan decided to try his hand as a baseball player. His baseball skillset was '**valued**' completely different than his basketball skillset, and thus, he was sent to the baseball minor league and paid 'minor' money strictly based on his baseball technical skill-set (he was a horrible baseball player, needless to say).

How is it that 'the greatest' player of all time in one aspect, basketball, and one company (The Chicago Bulls) earning an income of up to $36 million per year, could be paid just $850 a month in another sport?

In baseball, Michael Jordan **brought no real value. There** was no such thing as job security for even Michael Jordan, as they never won games or championships **because of his skill sets**, and his income in baseball reflected this.

Life Lesson 10

Why You Make What You Make

"You get paid for bringing value to the marketplace," Jim Rohn.

To be clear, bringing '**value**' to a business means 1 of 3 things:

1. You help the business **make more money** (largely through selling or improving their products or services).
2. You help the business **save more money**.
3. You help the business **save time** by running more efficiently and effectively, i.e. improving the business model in some aspect.

If you want to earn more, contribute more of what **your company values**.

A business is not built to make you a millionaire. It is like driving a car and expecting it to fly after it hits a certain speed. You get paid based on the types of problems you solve. What value do you bring to your current employer? For the most part, your paycheck is a large reflection of how 'valued' your skillsets are to your current employer. Simply put, if you can solve and manage more valuable problems, they'd probably pay you more money; however, it is extremely important to point out that the type of problems you're solving are a high enough priority for your company.

For example, fixing a printer for a company may not be that important to a company, though it is a 'valued' skill set, but creating, establishing, and executing a plan that will install 1,000 printers across your company's different locations across the country may be seen as solving a higher problem, and thus, pay you more.

If you sold 20-30% more products for your company, do you think they would increase your income, as a result of you adding more income for them? If I 'Googled' your industry, would you appear in the search results? Those years that you put in becoming an expert at what you do, absolutely matter.

When I first left the military, I was once working at a well-known telecommunications company in the Atlanta area, and I was making around $50k a year. I was new to IT at the time and had been working my way to building relationships within the workplace. And since I was in IT, the perception can be that you must be a 'little' smart to work in technology. As time went on, I got along great with everyone and for the large part, felt respected for my contributions, intellect, and ability to solve technical problems.

At some point, I had to fix a computer for someone in accounting and saw the salary sheet. My human curiosity kicked in, and my eyes were immediately drawn to the very top where I saw that the CEO was earning **$20,000,000+** a year…

As a military veteran, it was normal for everyone's salaries to be public as our salaries were funded by taxpayer dollars. However, there is usually a large bit of 'secrecy' in the civilian world as to who's earning what.

Now had this individual earned double my salary, no issues on my part.

Had this individual been earning triple my salary, no issues on my part.

Had this individual been earning 4x my salary, no issues on my part.

But +100x what I was earning…

It wasn't like this individual was superhuman,

He wasn't a famous athlete and maybe wasn't even the smartest person in the room at times (and I say that with no disrespect intended).

Didn't make straight A's in high school.
Didn't attend an Ivy League school.

It really hit me hard because it popped several beliefs of mine:

1. No ivy league
2. That you had to be the smartest person in the room.
   a. A majority of the employees had a master's degree.
   And even if this person was the smartest guy in the room, I knew countless intellectuals who weren't earning that much income.
3. You didn't need to work 60-70 hours a week to necessarily 'earn more'.

I began asking around to see if it was normal for a CEO to earn this sort of income, and the reaction was largely yes; it's normal.

This, for the large part, was an average guy.

We both worked 5 days a week, 8-10 hours a day, 40-50 hours a week.

I had heard that this person was even a 'C' Student in high school; and so he naturally wasn't a good student; he **had to become one**.

If you're going to work 40 hours a week, because, for the most part, you may have to do this for survival, why not put yourself in a position to earn the most?

Why not make the most of your 40-hour workweek? To make the most of your time?

I realized that they liked me, I realized that they loved me, I realized that they respected me, but I knew that my 'skillset' wasn't that critical to the business; therefore, I knew at that moment, I had to up my game and lift my skillset (mostly through self-education).

My education, my certifications, my experience, my technical skillset and the problems I was solving were not that valued **at that company (in that position)**.

"You earn what you believe you're worth," Connie Podesta.

One way to earn more or to actually reflect why you make what you make is to determine the amount of value you bring to a business and or its customers. There is a phenomenal business book entitled, "The Personal MBA," in which author, John Kaufman, brilliantly brings down the four ways to increase a business's revenue:

1. "Increase the number of customers you serve.
2. Increase the average size of each transaction by selling more.
3. Increase the frequency of transactions per customer.
4. Raise your prices."

If you significantly contributed to one of these four areas, in time, the business would reflect this in your salary. It's also worth pointing out, but in a lot of cases your income isn't necessarily attached to the outcome. So if the company sells $100m+ you may not see more than a significant bonus and not necessarily a permanent pay increase going forward; which again, isn't necessarily a bad thing, you just need to understand how and why the ***business model*** works the way it does.

How well do you know the business you've worked for in the last 1, 2, 5+ years? Could you describe in detail how every department works? Do you truly understand how your company earns money?

Many people will declare that they earn what they earn based on their race, gender, religion, politics (who's in office), "the man," your family's social status, whether they attended private or public school, & your level of formal education.

Let's look at those who earn between a certain amount and why they earn that amount:

~$1-100k: typically provide solutions (value) to problems (a job) within their direct community, neighborhood or **department within the company they work.**

~$100-$250k: typically provide solutions (value) to problems (a job) within their direct community, neighborhood or **company's managerial level and higher.**

~$500k-$1m: typically provide solutions (value) to problems within their direct community, neighborhood, city, state, or regional; as well as company level **nationwide.**

~$1M: typically provide solutions (value) to problems within their direct community, neighborhood, city, state, national and **international or company (internationally)**.

~$1B+: Bill Gates, Mark Zuckerberg, Steve Jobs, all provided solutions (value) to **GLOBAL** problems; it's why they're billionaires. For the large part, billionaires solve a common problem that **everyone on the planet** can essentially relate to.

--Bill Gates was the first person to make computer operating systems communicate with one another, so if you've ever used a computer in your lifetime, thank Bill Gates.

--Steve Jobs created the first *user-friendly*, feature enriched smartphone, so if you've ever used a smartphone in your lifetime, thank Steve Jobs.

--Mark Zuckerberg is one of the richest people on the planet because he **solved a global problem**, not because he went to Harvard (we all saw the movie, he infamously dropped out of Harvard). Zuckerberg is the first person in the world to create a ***global, user-friendly database***. Before Facebook, we all had to wait for the 500 pages 'Yellow Pages' phone book to be delivered on our doorstep once a year. Now, we can type in an old friend, family member, or classmate into Facebook and connect with them instantly; this is essential because you could not do this (**on a global scale**) before a 23-year-old Zuckerberg solved this global problem.

(*NOTE: I'm not advocating on behalf of Facebook's business practices, but simply highlighting Zuckerberg's **initial** vision to solve a problem on a mass scale).

If you haven't solved problems on a global scale, it's why you're not a billionaire.

    Solving problems (bring value) at both a lower and higher level through **providing simple solutions to common problems we all have** i.e. food, water, and shelter.
    Think of the **impact** the traffic app, 'Waze' has had on your community. How many people utilize this app because it helps them be more effective in traffic? What about the resourcefulness of apps like 'Uber' or 'Lyft'? What do you think it's founders/creator net worth is as a result of creating resourceful solutions that millions (potentially billions) of people utilize, **daily**?
    Doctors, mechanics, lawyers, and engineers can charge you $50-500 an hour, not because they solved or identified the problem in 10-15 minutes, but because of their combined *education, certification, and 'years' of experience* that allowed them to accurately identify the problem important to you.
    Those years that you put in becoming an expert at what you do, absolutely matter.

The 'business' of jasketball:

It may be a fair comparison, as both Lebron James and Earvin 'Magic' Johnson are (or were) not only at the top of the NBA, from a skillset standpoint, but were largely the face of the league (business) as well. However, if you compare their career earnings on the court, the difference is absolutely astounding.

*Earvin 'Magic' Johnson total NBA Career earnings: **$18 million** (13 years)

*Lebron James total NBA Career earnings: **$387.2 million** (By the end of the 2021-2022 season, he'll have earned per Spotrac, which tracks athlete salaries.) (17+ years)

*Note: This is strictly NBA contract earnings, not endorsements, or privately owned businesses

It's not that LeBron James is a better basketball player than Magic Johnson, as Magic has 5 championships to Lebron's 3 (for now); but the business of the NBA now has a larger market i.e., more customers to 'serve' via the numerous platforms from cable TV, social media, streaming services, websites, and summer touring leagues or tournaments held across the globe (as they're no longer just in the US). There was largely none of this in the '70-'90s when Magic Johnson played and the salaries between the generations reflect this.

As of 2019, the NBA has a **combined total annual salary** of **$3,672,772,340.00** to its **450 players**. For the 2018-19 season, the average NBA salary is $6,388,007, per Basketball-Reference. *The business* of the NBA has grown tremendously, and they are allowed to serve their customers more of what they want, in numerous ways possible.

You are a business professional.
You are a business professional.
You are a business professional.

The reality is we are all business professionals, who specialize in something. *You will own a business or work for one.* Why not legitimately try to master, understand, and navigate, **business effectively**? Everything is a business or a business transaction. I'm always amused by the college student who hasn't 'decided' what their major is going to be, as I can't help but think, regardless if you want to be an eSports gamer, construction worker, Wall Street banker, music executive, or chef, **anything and everything, is a business**; therefore, why not major (or at least minor) in *business*? You'll either own a business or work for a business.

How many books on business have you read this week, month, and year? How many business seminars and or business conferences have you attended? You should be studying and preparing to run your own business.

To further expand on the book, The Personal MBA, it's author, Josh Kaufman, also breaks down the five parts of every business:

1. "Creates and delivers something of value...
2. That other people want or need...
3. At a price, they're willing to pay...
4. In a way that satisfies the customer's needs and expectations...
5. So that the business brings in enough profit to make it worthwhile for the owners to continue to operate..."

He goes on to say, that, *"every business is fundamentally a collection of 5 processes, each of which flows into the next:*

A. <u>Value creation</u>: *discovering what people want or need, and creating it.*
B. <u>Marketing</u>: *attracting attention & building demand for this creation.*
C. <u>Sales</u>: *turning prospective customers into paying customers.*
D. <u>Value Delivery</u>: *coming through on your promises to customers.*
E. <u>Finance</u>: *bringing in enough money to keep going and being worth it."*

I challenge you to **develop your own 'side hustle' in which you are the CEO of your own business** (for economic safety for your family). When you are on the clock, you should be trying to help grow that business for your employer **because you are essentially becoming a student of how to one day do it solo.**

"Small ideas keep you small…" ~the guru.

Think of it like this, every building you've ever walked into is a business.
The neighborhood hospital is a business.
The neighborhood elementary school is a business.
The local state college is a business.
The grocery store is a business.
The mall is a business.
The homeless shelter is even a 'non-profit' business.
Your home, apartment, condo, is even a business.

(*Don't pay the rent, mortgage, or taxes and see how long your local bank, city, or county will let you stay there, on *their* land).

Every website is a business. What do you think the '.com' stands for? Commercial, as in commercial organization. There's a joke that says, every time you click the mouse to enter a website, someone is getting paid.

How do we know this?

Every building had to be thought of, believed in, designed, and physically built. Resources were then required to bring the building to life, i.e. construction crew hired, building materials purchased, electricity, plumbing, heating/air, etc.

More than anything, there is almost always a staff that requires a wage for services rendered to the business. And of course, the land that the building sits on must be paid for to the bank which owns that real estate.

A business is a system, a process that repeatedly provides goods and services in exchange for money, and since everything is a business (transaction), you must strive to be a student (valedictorian) of business.

What's your plan to earn more and contribute more?
What's your plan to impact the company's bottom-line?
What's your plan to grow your skillset to ultimately impact your community?
What's your plan to grow your business acumen?
What's your plan to potentially own your own business, for your family's sake?

Moreover, once that plan is established **by you**, how much time in the 168 hours will you spend following your own plan? If you were to audit your time in the seven days, would most of your time be dedicated to the plan you created?

How to produce more income:

You can earn more income when you begin to **solve problems for people.** Look for problems to solve in your neighborhood, chances are they're the same problems in your city, state, country, and maybe even globally.

You are an expert in something. Whether you've been working for 1, 2, 5, or 10+ years, you have experience in something that people (a business) is willing to compensate you for. Ideally, you can align with 'what you're good at' with what you love to do; therefore, why not set yourself up as an 'expert' or leader in that field?

To be seen as an expert, you have to 'market yourself' (or sell yourself) as an expert. **You need to build your own brand.** It's how the market sees us. *Personal Branding* expert, Matt Wilson, said it best, "Our brand is our reputation, which is built upon our stories and expertise, and our willingness to share our knowledge.

Here are 6 key ways to become known as an expert in your field:

1. Become social. "It's **not social media, it's business media**," Kendall Ficklin.
2. Speak publicly in or around your field at events, trade shows, and conferences.
3. Write a blog.
4. Write your book.

5. Run a workshop or webinar.
6. Network online and offline."

Market your skillset: if there was a problem in your industry, how many people would think of *looking for you* to come and solve it? Again, I ask, if someone 'googled' your industry, would you even show up in the search results on page one?

"It's not what you know, it's not who you know, **it's who knows you.**" ~Some Smart Dude on the Internet.

Ask your direct manager what the 3 biggest issues are in your department:

(With permission) ask his or her boss what the 3 biggest issues are at the next level.

(With permission) continue asking up to the level of the CEO (or c-suite).

Research, study, and identify 3 legitimate solutions to **each** of these problems, and be sure to think about **how to** successfully implement them, providing real strategies.

Point being that, if you want to earn more income, start by solving real problems that matter, **on the next level**. Solve, manage, and come up with solutions to problems that impact your **entire** company, not just your department.

"be the best at a particular industry; this opens new opportunities… the market will find you," Dr. Dennis Kimbro.

The best way to max out your earning potential is to take your intellectual property (your knowledge, skills, and abilities) of one main area, i.e. accounting, taxes, IT, or women's hair and **post it or provide it online** because **the Internet never closes** and the 1 billion people, customers, and clients can always access your content (your ideas, your gift, and your abilities); that you are providing them that can enhance their life (or business) in some way, shape, or form, as a solution.

*Bonus point:

Did you know that Jeff Bezos (as of 2019 the wealthiest man on the planet) is not the highest-paid employee at his own company, Amazon? "*Amazon Web Services is a cloud powerhouse, a more than $12 billion enterprise. So it's no surprise that Amazon is rewarding the man in charge of AWS, its CEO Andy Jassy. Jassy received approximately $35.6 million in total compensation in 2016, according to a filing with the U.S. Securities and Exchange Commission disclosed Wednesday,*" (www.geekwire.com).
Bezos' fortune came because he not only founded Amazon but is the largest shareholder of the prized stock.

What's your life plan to earn more income for your future and your family?

There is a saying, "stay at least one year to learn, two years to grow, three years to count, and four years to run a big piece of the place,"
~Some Smart Dude on the Internet.

Multiple Streams of Income

This one stings because I am always concerned that people may miss the point, but as previously stated, a job is largely meant to maintain you, **not make you rich**. You do not own that job, the company does; but you do **own** your career. You must have more than one skill (for economic safety) because you have no guarantee that your job, company, or industry will be there tomorrow. 7 October 2019, Fortune 500 powerhouse, GE, announced, "General Electric announced Monday it will **freeze its US pension plan for about 20,000 workers** to help clean up the company's beleaguered balance sheet," (WallStreetJournal.com).

How do these 20,000 employees cover the mortgage, pay for any emergency medical expenses, or know that dinner is covered for the next few weeks? For my younger friends, a pension plan is essentially a monthly payment guaranteed once you work a specific period of time for a company i.e. 5 years. Many employees committed years of their lives to a business with the promise or guarantee that would have a strong source of income coming for the remainder of their lives and they're not wrong to lean on this, but the bank or grocery stores do not want to hear any sad stories. If you need or want their services (medical, food, or a financial loan) you must pay for that (it's a business transaction) **and everything is a business.**

"Some 380,000 federal employees from nine departments and several smaller agencies have been forced to go on furlough because of the government shutdown, which is now in its 26th day – the longest in U.S. history. While another 420,000 employees – many in public-safety positions – **are working without pay** mainly because their jobs are considered essential. They were assured of back pay once the shutdown is over," www.usatoday.com

There are estimated to be over 3.5 million truck drivers in the United States. As of 2019, Tesla, a company that is mass-producing self-driving and electric cars and semi-truck are taking the world by storm. Its' founder, Elon Musk, is largely seen as a disruptor of industries, and they have been working on a self-driving semi-truck for the future. Let's look:

> *"Grocery giant Albertsons is buying 10 Tesla Semi trucks and plans to operate them in Southern California…*
> *Also dozens of companies [are] putting down a minimum of $20,000 per truck to get on Tesla's pre-order list. Albertson's likely paid at least $200,000 to pre-order 10 trucks.*
> *Other early Semi backers include Memphis-based FedEx Corp., Pepsi, Anheuser-Busch, Walmart Inc, Mei-*

jer, United Parcel Service Inc., DHL, Sysco Corp., and Ryder System Inc.
FedEx ordered 20 Tesla Semis in March," (www.bizjournals.com, 2018).

So, what does the future hold for the 3.5 million truck drivers whose sole income may largely come from truck driving? What happens if (*or when*) their jobs are outsourced to a self-driving truck?

They have also just announced a robot that can now produce 300 pizzas an hour, point being; there is no such thing as job security.

There will always be situations in your life when you will need more than one source of income for you and your family. Your goal should be to match part-time with what you make full time. A recession, layoffs, a government shutdown is almost a guarantee (and in some instances) necessary to shake off some illegitimate 'financial gains' in the course of 5-10 years.

The real point of the board game, Monopoly, was to show you how to 'cash out' and more importantly, to show that at no point when you roll the dice are you to 'work 40 hours' for 40 years to earn money. Every opportunity was to buy a business and or piece of property (real estate).

The point of Monopoly:

- Was not to 'brag' about your salary.
- Was not to stay in the rat race forever.
- It never said roll the dice and go to college and get a major you hate.

The point of Monopoly **was to teach you to establish multiple streams of income, largely through ownership (own a business or own real estate).**

The legendary game was designed to teach you to buy and collect businesses and real estate so that as you go through 'life' you are prepared for **what will come your way** and ultimately, to have enough established enough, so that you may 'cash out' through becoming financially independent.

"Their vision is according to what they see. **We** [often] **only see time for money,**" said Jemal King, the '9-5 Millionaire' who owns over 100 properties and was a full-time police officer with the Chicago Police Dept. for close to 20 years and is still not even 50 years of age. His point is simple; when you typically work with a traditional company and have an hourly rate or an annual salary, **you're limited and capped by the number of hours in a day.** You cannot work past the 24 hours, and therefore, you can earn only so much in an 8, 12, or even 24-hour shift. You will ultimately run out of time in the day.

The reality is you will never have enough income, and you do not know which life hurdle is coming at you tomorrow, therefore, establishing some sort of ownership (either of a business or real estate) and more importantly, establishing multiple streams of income is vital for your economic safety.

Take into consideration the following scenarios:

-The newly retiree whose sole hope to survive is a pension, 401k, or mostly, social security.

-The military veteran(s) transitioning into civilian life who may be in between job opportunities.

-The newlywed couple with a baby on the way, who are scrounging for diapers, baby formula, and a suitable home for the newborn.

-The college student who hates school and doesn't know what they want to major in, but needs to pay the rent, food, and basics of life.

(*Think Kanye's College Dropout).

-How many people in your family (or extended family) have had a medical emergency and are unable to work, i.e. cancer, car accident, an extended stay in the hospital, etc.?

As previously mentioned, you should have a side hustle in which you are the CEO, and you actually own something outright. Wealthy people primarily create their wealth through either owning a business or owning real estate. Need proof? Here you go! Forbes lists that,"there are now 1,700 new millionaires **created every day** in America." Mathematically, 1,700 do not inherit millions, daily. Wealth is largely established through ownership, either of business or real estate.

Today, there are about 8 million American households with assets worth more than $1 million, excluding properties and luxury goods," (www.fortune.com). It goes without saying, but 8 million is not a small number. 8 million people are not lucky. 8 million people did not 'inherit' their wealth. 8 million people did not hit the lotto.

There is no excuse here.

Everybody works hard, there's no denying this, but not everybody *thinks* hard. It's not smart to take a $500-$1,200 'smartphone' (psst, it's really a computer) and play children's games with it (insert Angry Birds). There are thousands of websites, blogs, books (even audiobooks), that can and will teach you how to create a steady source of income, again, not to buy material items, but to set up and secure your family's financial well-being.

Here are a few ideas for initial ownership sources as well as the potential for passive income (for your family's future):

--*Rental property:*

Real estate is the #1 market for millionaires. You could start with a mobile home as they average between

$15,000-$65,000. For example, if you purchased a ranch or mobile home for $62,900 with a monthly 'mortgage' payment of $321 and an interest rate of 3.92%, it can be rented out for $500-$800 a month depending on the location. Keep in mind, we'd need 10-15% saved for maintenance and other issues but starting with something under $60,000 is completely doable; and potentially pocketing $200-300 a month is never a bad time, especially if we're not physically 'clocking' in somewhere 8 hours a day to earn it.

If you're anything like me, you hesitate to believe anything you see or hear, so check out the numbers yourself:

1st Property, $62,900	
Valdosta, Ga 31602	
Monthly Rent	$675.00
Monthly Expenses:	
Mortgage	$321.83
Small loan for Downpayment	$50-$125
Property Mgmt (10%)	$60.00
Taxes	$28.00
Home Insurance	$10.00
Savings for Repairs (5%)	$23.50
	$443.33
Monthly take home	$231.67
Annual take home	$2,780.04

$12,580 downpayment (20%)

https://www.mobilehomesell.com/mobile-home-prices/

Need down payment money for the property? Uber and Lyft for 6-18 months and make a goal of $1k a month in side income (that's just $33 a day). You don't have a car? Lyft has a leasing program in which they'll lease the car to you as long as you can make 25 trips in a week, that's basically 3-4 rides a day.

--*Create an online store.*
Do you ever notice how everything that you order from Amazon comes from a different 'shipper'? The reality is it all comes from a different 'online store'; which, theoretically is owned by someone like *you*.

If you can create and start a social media account, you can create an online store. Check out www.Shopify and www.Alibaba.com to get started. Shopify.com even has an online course built in to teach you how to get started with your store.

--*Write a book.*

The world needs to hear your story. If you can share your experience and help someone else who is struggling in an area, this is a 'win-win' situation. There's no reason you cannot or should not monetize your knowledge, skills, and experience. There was a purpose in your pain and there is a lane in monetizing your message.

--*Consult.*

Your years of experience simply matter. You can take what you know and help a local business grow in some capacity. You have to understand that if you've been in the same industry for three years, you're an expert. You are an expert in something. The millennial generation has an enormous advantage with social media, websites, and e-commerce as they've grown up with the Internet. Find three local 'mom-n-pop' businesses close to your home and sell your knowledge of social media (or whatever your strength(s)) to promote their business.

Try this line, "I'd like to **help you grow your business.** Would you be open to a possible partnership?"

You can also look at websites such as www.upwork.com and www.fiverr.com for online and remote side gigs through your new 'online company'. You can set up your own Limited Liability Corporation (LLC), in minutes via www.legalzoom.com

***Pro-tip:**

This cannot be overstated, I understand that many people live in small towns that may appear to have limited resources nearby; however, if you're reading or listening to this book on a smartphone then you probably have access to the **world wide web.** That 'www' you enter before every website, means that you have access to people across the globe as the Internet itself is a 'network,' which means you can communicate with other people and exchange information, ideas, and more importantly, solutions to your problems.

Again, the goal should be to match part-time with what you make full time for you, your family, and your future. The point here is simple; we are constantly exchanging our money for products and services (remember, everything is a business). Let's get on the other side of the cash register and not to 'get money', but to 'get opportunities' for the impending hurdles life will bring us. *You will never have enough* income to protect you, your family, and your future.

The Internet was designed to educate, communicate, and share information. We can put our ideas, thoughts, knowledge, experiences, skills, and abilities together and overcome any man-made obstacle; but we continue to focus on celebrities, sports, and music with one of the most powerful tools ever created. I've never met anyone who made $1 streaming Netflix.

You can build or you can bull$hit, it's on you.

****

Nothing irritates me more than walking into a business and seeing someone on their phone while they're on the clock. This especially happens when the business is 'slow', and they're not particularly busy. I can't help but think; you're there to grow in many aspects, so why not help grow the business? If you're there and on your phone, why not promote the business? This could bring tremendous value to a business, especially a smaller 'mom-n-pop' business. Facebook gets an estimated 1 billion users a day on its website. They'll pay you more if you truly and consistently contributed to the business's 'bottom-line' (earned them more money or saved them more money).

69.5 Syndrome:

I'm going to take you back to school, so bear with me, but do you remember when the teacher would hand back the graded tests or exams, and someone would get a 95, another student a 90, 85, or 80, and that one person would get a 69.5 rounded up to a 70 and would be just enough to pass? This often feels like what we do when we settle. School was a definite struggle for me, as I could never truly understand the point of taking the 'unnecessary' courses i.e. anything chemistry, calculus, and physics (and to be fair, I've yet to use the periodic table in the workforce); but a lot of the point in school

The Mediocre Miracle

was to *develop your work habits, patterns, and discipline to carry out responsibility* and tasks.

The teacher is like a boss giving you instructions, sometimes you do not want to do them and do not understand why it is important.

School helps to shape your contribution to the workforce, but much like the student, me, who barely passed with a 69.5 took this same bare minimum effort of studying into the workforce. Early in my career, I was paid just enough to not quit and in return, I would work just hard enough to not get fired.

The point here is some of you show up to work with the Squidward mentality and not SpongeBob's, and it is reflected in your paycheck. If you do not contribute more (to your job, company, community, environment), you will not earn more.

#DontBeSquidward

Sales & Negotiation:

"You don't get paid your worth; you get paid what you negotiate.".
~Some Smart Dude on the Internet

1. It legitimately took me 37 years to realize this, but 'sales' is a 'technical skill-set', which all business professionals, i.e. **you**, absolutely need!
   (*Remember, you'll either work for a business or own one).
   You're selling yourself every time you walk in a room and contribute to a conversation.
2. Everything is negotiable; therefore, **never take the first offer.**
3. "You earn what you believe you're worth," Connie Podesta.

Thank you for coming to my TED Talk.

Have more than one skill:

A business has several key components or departments, why not master more than one? As a key note to remember, everything is a business (a process) and more importantly, there is no such thing as job security.

- ✓ Sales
- ✓ Marketing
- ✓ Finance/Accounting

- ✓ Human Resources
- ✓ Executive Management
- ✓ Business Operations
  - IT
  - Logistics
  - Production

I used to sell myself as a guy who can fix PCs. I started studying the G.O.A.T.S. (greatest of all times) of the technology industry and adjusted my thinking, my angle, and my perception from,

"help me...hire me, please" to "allow me to partner with you and allow me to help you. Please let me show you how technology can improve your bottom-line."

Let me help you, your business, and ultimately, your bottom-line.

Much love to Professor Dennis Kimbro from Clark Atlanta University for helping me adjust my aim.

I hate to harp on business, finances, and career, but the reality is it is such an impactful portion of all of our lives; and specifically, I see so many people struggle with their personal mission, career, and lack of life purpose or fulfillment from their career choice; however, I'd like to finally point out the significance of your 'life's work'.

We were not put here with the sole purpose of collecting money, which is *man-made*. Your life, efforts, and example can *essentially help another human being in some capacity*. You have the ability to light someone else's candle. Once you find your true lane, you have the potential to change someone's life and ultimately, impact their mind, body, & soul.

It is because of this that you need to make one last mental shift. You see **you, yourself are your own business**, a Limited Liability Corporation, (LLC).

It has always been **'You, LLC'**.

You, LLC.

*You are your own brand. *
You are your own business.

You need to understand, acknowledge, and know that you are always in the business of selling yourself; this is exactly what your resume is. Your resume is a document in which you are selling your technical skillset(s).
"Each person's income is determined by their personal philosophy," Jim Rohn.

You largely have to work 8 hours a day anyway, **why not put yourself in a position to earn the most and maximize** your 8 hours away from your family? What is your personal philosophy (life plan)? Some individuals think it is the job of their parents, high school, college, to teach them everything they need to know in life. How can you advance your personal philosophy? Do you have one? How much of it involves increasing your technical skillsets? Why do you not dare to build out your dream? You have to work anyway? Why not work towards owning your dream?

What is your long-term game?
What is your legacy?
What do you want them to say in your eulogy?

Your game plan, You, LLC should be so big that it seems impossible to build as "It's not what the dream is, it's what the dream does," said the Guru. Creating and establishing your vision **will grow you into who you need to become.**

In other words, if there is no dream, you're probably not growing dude.

Life Lesson 11

The Mediocre Miracle

It's amazing to go to a zoo or circus and watch the animals of various shapes and sizes and what takes place there. I once saw an animal trainer at a circus **control** six lions in a cage with nothing more than a whip. I've seen an animal trainer control, dominate, and lead a family of elephants to sit and obey. I've seen tigers sit up on bar stools and pretend to be as passive as a house cat.

I'm always confused because I can't tell if this is amazing or sad to see the 'King of the Jungle' behave like the court jester. How can something as strong as the lion (especially when there are six lions to one trainer in a cage) pretend to have no power, authority, or control?

Like animals in a zoo, some of us have been programmed, trained, and crafted to not step into or recognize our greatness. The individual who works 8 hours a day, 40 hours a week often looks defeated as he or she shows up continuously to the life that he or she created and shows no power, authority, or control over their life.

However, much like the elephant or lion chained in a circus, we have been programmed, trained, and crafted out of our creative greatness. Do you notice how an animal at the zoo usually looks depressed? Dolphins in captivity have their fins fall over, elephants look frail, tigers/lions look like domesticated house cats, or the individual who works 8 hours a day, and 40 hours a week looks defeated in a career they have no passion for.

We have been distracted from our own greatness.

So, I will ask one final time, **who have you decided to become**?

What is your life plan?

Where and whom will you decide and declare to be in the next 12, 24, 36, 48 months?

If you don't have a written game plan, let's create one. Be detailed, but note, this does not mean career only! You are designing, creating, writing your legacy; be big, be bold, be so scared to say it out loud, and to write it down, but have it excite you enough that you'll commit to finishing it.

Do you understand that you are built and not born?

What are you doing, and **where are you going?**

Those were just my thoughts and self-reflection at my own failures and shortcomings…

You have to understand though that you becoming more is also not really about you, but being the example for others in your circle. How many people in your circle could you help if they saw you on your 'A' game consistently? You cannot help someone if you're strug-gling right alongside them.

"You're powerful beyond measure…" ~anonymous.

Just a reminder of your capabilities as a human being on what you can accomplish; if the sky's the limit, then why are there footprints on the moon?

"Pay attention to the things you are naturally drawn to. They are often connected to your path, passion, and purpose in life. Have the courage to follow them," Ruben Chavez

This is why you stop and stare at the sunrise or sunset.

This is why you stop and stare at the mountains in the backdrop of Colorado.

This is why you stop and stare at a full moon.

This is why you stop and stare at the stars.

This is why every time you see the ocean, that first glance, takes your breath away…

Mother Nature is the ultimate reminder, it is like look-ing into a magnifying glass or as if you're looking into the ultimate reflection of who you could be or who you should be.

It's the ultimate display of your potential and it's too powerful, too beautiful to ignore. This is why some say that the 'water is calling me'; it is whispering to you to step into your true potential. Mother Nature is simply your mirror.

With the right training, mentor, coaching, support group, role models to give you the guidance and structure you need (insert Gary V.), with the right plan or strategy, you can become more than you imagine. And by 'the right mentor or coach', I truly mean, be a student of a legitimate and proven subject matter expert; do not be a student of someone spreading their 'barbershop-wisdom'. You know the type, the "if that was me, I would…"kind of "experts" and you find out this individual has no experience of any kind on the subject but somehow deems their opinion is not only valid but necessary.

What is distracting you from you, and what are *they* selling you? Often it is the idea that you, alone, are not enough…

We have the power to become more. My question is **why isn't growing into the greatest version of ourselves the most important focus** of our lives? Not out of greed of money or to attain material possessions, but to help inspire our friends, family, community, and maybe the world. So many of us, myself included, have become distracted. The simple idea, belief system, or story we tell ourselves of who we aren't.

You, me, we, were not put here to 'secure the bag', collect the check, make 6 figures, or become a millionaire. We were put here to grow, learn, and become more and evolve into our true potential so that we can essentially inspire one another to do the same.

Take a look at this question by Dr. Eric Thomas – "Who is missing out because you're not walking in your dream?"

There is no such thing as a mediocre miracle. How can any human, a living breathing miracle, be mediocre? It can be proven that we are all miracles.

Regardless of your race, religion, or cultural backgrounds, let's take into consideration how we are all brought into the world. When a man and woman decide to produce a child, 1 seed out of millions is joined with 1 egg and 9 months later, a healthy baby is born. This is a miraculous process, and we just take for granted.

We are all physically able to breathe on our own, that is a miracle, as some cannot.

You may be able to see on your own, that is a miracle, as some cannot.

You may be able to hear on your own, that is a miracle, as some cannot.

You may be able to walk on your own, that is a miracle, as some cannot.

You may be able to talk on your own, that is a miracle, as some cannot.

You have **the ability to think on your own**, that is a miracle.

You woke up this morning, that is a miracle, as some will not.

The Mediocre Miracle

The Center for Disease Control states that 225,000 die every day across the globe, totaling 25,000,000 humans that don't live to see the end of the year, so the fact that you are alive and breathing today, is a miracle. The very fact that you can breathe on our own without the assistance of an oxygen tank, is a miracle. If you do not believe me, please visit your nearest hospice and see how many people are clinging to an oxygen tank to breathe for them. As soon as the oxygen tank is turned off, they may pass.

Scientists have found that at the molecular level, all living components consist of what is referred to as the 'Building Blocks of Life,' being Hydrogen, Oxygen, Carbon, and Nitrogen. Apparently, these four compounds are also found in the Sun, Moon, and Stars. This is amazing to know that essentially, **we are filled with the same foundation as what powers the Sun, Moon, and Stars.**

We are all essentially, stardust…

It is mesmerizing that in our core, we can 'glow' like the Moon…

In our being, we can shine like the Sun…

It makes me wonder, are we staring at the Sun, Moon, and Stars in amazement or have they been staring at us in amazement…

but we've all been distracted from our own greatness.

We have been distracted from our mindset, heart-set, and soul-set.

In the now instant classic Marvel movie, Black Panther, there is an incredible display of technology used. In many scenes, they have the ability to use a hologram to see and hear people who are not physically standing in front of them, almost 'Facetime' in the future. I wish I could use this same technology to essentially reach into your chest, pull out your heart, and show you via hologram, '*you*', at your full potential. This is the '*you*' embedded in your heart. This is the '*you*' at your best. This is the '*you*' that you were designed to be. This is the '*you*' that we all need to set as the benchmark. This '*you*' walks different, talks different, and is seen, different. Your highest self.

"It's time for you to be, who we need you to be," Moana's Dad whispered (*to all of us*).

-The ultimate oxymoron:

> We have all been, in some way or aspect of our life, mediocre and yet to be born and live, breathe, and walk this Earth, we truly are miracles. If we are miracles, we cannot be mediocre, as that would be the ultimate oxymoron. We all have the potential to become more.

"Your talent is God's gift to you. What you do with it is your gift back to God," Leo Buscaglia.

My goal with this book was to essentially challenge not only what's in your head, but what's in your heart. My hope is that you are confidently able to see and realize your true power.

I believe in you.

I've never been an overly religious person, but I do try and see and feel God in every heart. We all see skin color, but if you try, you can feel someone's heartbeat. This is my gift and my curse. I see people for who they could be and who they should be; all of us, at our absolute best; and I cannot help but feel and truly know that **we are all miracles.**

The Mediocre Miracle.

Assessment:

I invite you to take some legitimate time to access the different areas of your life. On a scale from 1-10 (1 being the lowest, 10 being amazing) grade yourself on each area of your life. Then let's establish 3 goals in each area so that we can improve here. If we utilize the Rule of 168 correctly (and maximize our 168 hrs. in a week) and take real steps, create action plans, and focus on these goals, they can be achieved.

Quality of Life: Overall	Self Education	Personal Relationships	Mind, Body & Soul	Financial Indep.	Prof. Career	Formal Education
Current Grade, 1-10:						
Goal 1 to aim for						
Goal 2 to aim for						
Goal 3 to aim for						

The Mediocre Miracle

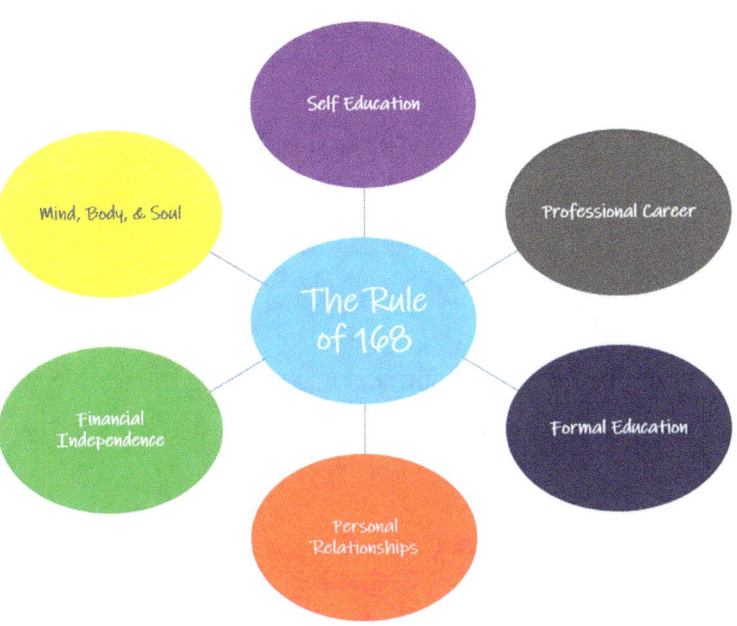

Resources:

If you'd like help, assistance, or coaching please feel free to reach out via our website so we can discuss clarity & a strategy plan for your pain points.

www.themediocremiracle.com
www.ritchiethomas.com/coaching

To book Ritchie R Thomas for your next event, conference, or training session(s) please contact:

info@ritchiethomas.com

Additional workshops/programs include:

- How to Successfully Transition Out of the Military

- The Rule of 168 Workshop (Time & Productivity Management Tool)

- Military Leadership Training ("Is My Unit Better Because I Lead It" & "Am I Preparing My Soldiers for Life After the Uniform")

Resources:

I also would like to point to some reading material that I have turned to in my downtimes to reprogram the way that I think and have been extremely resourceful to me.

<u>Personal Relationships</u>: The 5 Love Languages
<u>Finances</u>: Dave Ramsey's 'Financial Peace Univ.', Rich Dad Poor Dad
<u>Mind, Body, & Soul</u>: The Bible
<u>Mind</u>: The Monk Who Sold His Ferrari, Can't Hurt Me
<u>Body</u>: Bigger, Leaner, Stronger
<u>Soul</u>: The 4 Truths, As a Man Thinketh
<u>Formal Education</u>: 2-3 books based upon your interest, gift(s), or major
    <u>Self Education</u>: Think & Grow Rich, Tools of Titans
<u>Professional Career</u>: The Wealth Choice
    <u>Business</u>: The Personal MBA

The Mediocre Miracle

I would also like to share some 'online' coaches, mentors, and teachers that I have leaned on to grow in these various areas as well.

Quality of Life: Overall	Self Education	Personal Relation-ships	Mind, Body & Soul	Financial Indep.	Prof. Career	Formal Education
Coaches/ Mentor	Jim Rohn	Dr. Kevin Leman	Wayne Dyer	Dave Ramsey	Gary Vaynerchuk	Dr. Michael E. Dyson
	Robin Sharma	Gary Smalley	Alan Watts	Warren Buffett	Simon Sinek	Dr. Dennis Kimbro
	Earl Nightingale	Sadghuru	Dr Eric Thomas	Robert Kiyosaki	Neville Goddard	Fred. Douglass
	Tony Robbins	Deepak Chopra	TD Jakes	Suze Orman	John Maxwell	Dr. Cornell West
		Brendan Burchard	Lisa Nichols	Les Brown	Chris Hogan	Top 3 in your career on Linkedin	Marcus Garvey

About the Author

Ritchie is an honorary ATLien with a salt-water heart still in Charleston, SC.

He was fortunate enough to have put on the military uniform for 6 years, where he was trained to push himself and others while learning a great sense of inner pride in belonging to something that was deeper than the dollar. He's survived through a combat zone in Afghanistan, jumped out of airplanes, hit 15 countries (35 if we count Epcot), & survived 3 hurricanes.

His gift is helping military servicemembers grow and helping them adjust from a soldier's mindset to a business professional's mindset.

He lives in Atlanta with his son, who thinks he's a full-time wrestler, his daughter who enjoys shooting him in the neck with NERF guns, the most world's most loyal cat (who thinks he's part tiger), & his beautiful wife of 15 years.

He remains fiercly loyal to House Lannister.

www.ingramcontent.com/pod-product-compliance
Lightning Source LLC
Chambersburg PA
CBHW071402290426
44108CB00014B/1652